EQUUSOLOGY

EQUUSOLOGY

DECIPHERING HUMAN AND HORSE TYPOLOGY

Melisa Pearce and Carolyn Fitzpatrick

touched by a
Horse

TOUCHED BY A HORSE, INC.
Elizabeth, Colorado

This book is dedicated to the wonderful,
unique personalities of horses everywhere.

Shadow
1992–2015

Equusology
Deciphering Human and Horse Typology
By Melisa Pearce and Carolyn Fitzpatrick

The information contained in this book is not intended as a substitute for psychological counseling, medical advice, or any other professional advice. If such advice is required, the services of a competent professional should be sought.

ISBN: 978-0-9760415-8-0
LCCN: 2015910565

Printed in the United States of America

Touched by a Horse, Inc.
Elizabeth, Colorado
www.TouchedbyaHorse.com

Illustrations by Alice Griffin, GriffinAE100@gmail.com

Cover and interior design by Pratt Brothers Composition, LLC, www.PrattBrothersComposition.com

Manuscript edited by Melanie Mulhall, Dragonheart, www.DragonheartWritingandEditing.com

Table of Contents

⬤ PART 2   OUR HORSES!

Foreword

WHOA! WHERE DID THAT REACTION COME FROM? MOST OF US HAVE HAD AN experience that left us wondering why the horse did something that seemed so out of character. Was it pure obstinacy, disobedience, or confusion? After all, you feed him, groom him, and work with him. You have learned about natural horsemanship methods, but you still feel that you and your horse are often listening to different drummers. What's the deal?

The answers to these questions and many more are in this book. Equusology exposes the missing link that you have been searching for to cultivate a more rewarding relationship with your horse. Equusology is the study of human and horse typologies. Within our pages, you will find illustrations and explanations relating to what you have been observing, and now you will be able to justify your interactions with your horse.

This is the first book that explains the importance of knowing both your temperament and your horse's temperament. It also provides the keys to compatibility with your horse. No longer will you wonder why your horse seems to gaze around a huge area when you bring him to a location that is new to him. No longer will you be mystified by the fact that he walks partially towards you when you are at the gate, then stops to look at you before continuing on to join you. No longer will you be frustrated because he wants to act up when you school him for hours in the ring. No longer will you feel perplexed about what approach you should take when you want to expose your horse to a new skill.

For more than four decades, I have observed and raised horses. During that time, I have also trained them to regional and national levels of competition. During the last two decades, I have been passionate about dressage and long-distance trail. This type of interaction with horses led me to realize that they are not all alike. Quite the contrary. They have different needs and different learning styles.

My coauthor, Melisa Pearce, is a lifelong horsewoman who has shown and bred quality Quarter Horses and American Paint Horses for decades. Our daily interactions with our horses, combined with our strong, inquisitive minds and our dedication to bettering the lives of horses, led us to the combined commitment to this book. Owners are searching for answers to their many questions about why their horses do certain things, and at least some of those answers lie within this book.

I first met Melisa Pearce in 2009 at the Virginia Horse Extravaganza. I had been following her and reading some of her messages on the internet, so I decided to travel to the expo to meet her. It didn't take long for me to realize that Melisa is a visionary. She clearly saw how her knowledge could be shared with students so they could learn her equine gestalt methods to coach others, thereby transforming their lives. I enrolled in and became certified by the Touched by a Horse EGCM program.

Both Melisa and I were committed to telling the world that horses have personalities, just like humans. Humans can be evaluated to determine what their preferences are in certain areas. So can horses.

Melisa has extensive knowledge and experience using the Keirsey Temperament Sorter with her private clients and students, so she has explained the test and results in detail within this book. She has woven some stories into the text to bring the concepts down to earth and hold everyone's interest. I am fascinated by the idea that horses can be better understood if humans have a tool to evaluate them in a consistent way, so my contributions within these pages are the creation of the measuring device for horses' temperaments and supporting exercises that will help you validate the horse evaluation tool results. We also added some training tips for you to use after you discover your temperament and your horse's temperament.

The first part of this book offers you the opportunity to take the Keirsey Temperament Sorter and understand your results. It also provides some depth of explanation about the personality types identified in the sorter. You will gain insights into your preferences and the preferences of others. Those insights will help you understand how you differ from others and how your preferences influence your decisions and reactions with others every day. Remember, those "others" include your horse.

The remainder of the book is dedicated to providing you with the tools you need to evaluate your horse's personality. The Equusology Sorter will help you determine your horse's type. You will also find fun exercises to test the answers you gave in the sorter questionnaire and ideas that will help you support your horse's personality so the two of you can understand each other on a whole different level—a personal level.

Humans not only have preferences, we have degrees of preference that impact how we socialize, take in information, process that information, and view our world. My argument is that horses also have those degrees of preference, and now you have a measuring device to enlighten you on what they are. I believe my job as an owner is to identify and understand my horse's innate traits and then support his needs. I can tell you, firsthand, that there are few things more rewarding to horse owners than understanding their horses on a personal basis.

There are many excellent books available on natural horsemanship, equine nutrition, stable management, individual horse breeds, and the many disciplines that horses and humans partner in. But this book explains horse-human dynamics by applying the time-tested Keirsey Temperament Sorter and our newly created Equusology Sorter. With this information, you and your horse can better cocreate a relationship with one another that is enjoyable, satisfying, and intimate—a true human-equine partnership.

Melisa and I have opened our minds to the uniqueness of our horses and have applied these methods to our own relationships with both humans and horses. It has been life changing for us—and our horses—and we pray that it will be for you, too.

CAROLYN P FITZPATRICK,
MS in psychology and conflict transformation
The Horse Connection, LLC
Bellamy Farms
Amherst, Virginia
February 2015

Acknowledgments

First and foremost, we would like to thank David Keirsey for his book *Please Understand Me*, which inspired this journey. We are so grateful to have his permission to use the Keirsey Temperament Sorter (KTS) and materials for the writing of this book.

There were many generous supporters and friends who helped encourage us along the way. Thanks to all of the Touched by a Horse students and certified practitioners of Equine Gestalt Coaching, aka the TBAH Herd, who love this typology material. In particular, thank you Alice Griffin, Ashara Morris, Barbara Broxterman, BB Harding, Harriet Morton, Lisa Martin, Michelle Griffith, and Michelle Sidun for your contributions of case studies on your wonderful equine partners.

Our editor, Melanie Mulhall, wrangled this book project from its early state to the finished book. Thank you, Melanie. Through you, I have had the pleasure of working with professionals throughout the project. In every project I bring to you, your professionalism makes all the difference in our books and in the present moment experience of writing. Your deep friendship decorates my life beyond measure.

Dan and Jim Pratt, thank you for jumping in to rescue the design process when we had to shift design teams right at the moment the book was ready for interior and cover design. You kept the book consistent in feel with previous TBAH books and you managed to govern the flow while keeping it fun, which shows you are masters of design.

Thank you, Helena Mariposa, for slowing down and proofing this tongue twister.

And we give a shout out to Jerilyn Becker for reading the rough drafts and giving us helpful feedback.

Alice Griffin, thank you for your playful illustrations and happy spirit. As an EGC Certified Practitioner, I have loved being your teacher in our TBAH program. Working with you on this book was a sheer delight because it showed how deeply you understand both horses and this material.

Kim Beer and Diana Garland, we thank you for your photography of our head shots.

The bulk of this project was written at my Arizona Ranch, where Carolyn and I met to have quality time and focus for the project. Our ranch manager, Audrey, was incredibly generous. Thank you for running errands and caretaking for us so our writing could be uninterrupted.

We are fortunate women to have supportive and encouraging husbands. Thank you, Dane and Jim, for your love and generous spirits.

Both Carolyn and I (Melisa) have spent our lives with hundreds of horses, each with distinct personalities. To every one of you, thank you. You have taught us the importance of truly listening to you and seeing you as individuals. This book is for you.

PART ONE

Who Are We Really?

CHAPTER ONE

Celebrate Difference

SANDY WALKS INTO HER CLOSET AND HANGS UP HER JACKET IN THE SECTION of her closet assigned to hold jackets, blazers, and coats. Glancing at her blouses and noticing a cream one among the other cream and white tones, she selects it to pair with a fresh pair of sweat pants after her shower and puts her barn attire in the hamper.

After showering and dressing, Sandy selects the sealed containers in the refrigerator that contain the salad items from the farmers market she has already diced and sliced. She quickly prepares her lunch, restacks her magazines, and places her files in order. After sorting her mail, Sandy returns a few e-mails before her conference call. Working from home has been easier for her than working at the company office ever was. She can stay organized and seems to maintain a high level of energy. Her only contacts with her coworkers are through e-mail and on the daily staff conference call.

Tonight she will be having dinner with her best friend, Marnie, at their favorite place. She has already e-mailed her reservation for the table she likes. Somehow,

Marnie has talked her into a volunteer project for the local horse rescue. Marnie is one of those people involved in everything. Sandy is pulling together the statistics and data for Marnie to use in her presentation before the rescue group. The presentation is not for another two months, but Sandy will be happy to have the research crossed off her list.

Across town, Marnie arrives home from the barn and forgets to remove her boots before stepping into her apartment. The mud steps make her laugh at herself as she conjectures that they will be dry enough to vacuum in a few days. She rationalizes leaving it until then by reminding herself that she wanted to rent a shampooer anyway to give her carpets a good cleaning. Her phone rings and she answers it, greeting one of her many friends for a quick chat. She agrees to meet her friend for dinner, forgetting about her plans with Sandy. Squealing when she thinks to ask her friend what time it is and discovers that it is later than she realizes, she says she has to run. She is late for the company conference call—again.

While dialing in to the call, she realizes she is starving and looks in the fridge for something to eat. Nothing looks identifiable or edible so she noshes on some crackers while listening to the moderator. Each department chimes in on their work projects. Marnie is not sure where her work file is but she knows she can wing it. Everyone loves Marnie. Her charisma and outgoing personality always brighten the calls. The boss seems to overlook that Marnie does not have the details of her report ready and frequently comments on Marnie's forward thinking and imagination.

Sandy is also on the conference call and Marnie smiles as Sandy quietly gives her very detailed and precise report. The moderator asks her to speak a bit louder. It sounds as if Sandy is reading. Her work is very accurate and her approach methodical. The boss relies on Sandy a great deal, knowing she can always be counted on to be responsible.

The last fifteen minutes of the call are dedicated to something the boss calls "idea factory." Anyone is allowed to contribute any idea or vision they may have for the company and its products. Marnie always livens up for that part of the call. Sandy has never spoken up, even though she has good ideas, but she sometimes tells Marnie about her ideas because she knows Marnie will present them.

After the call, Marnie spends some time playing with her cat and then sets off in search for her files to begin work. Maybe they are under the Sunday paper, which is spread around her living room, or maybe they are in her office area. They could even be in her car. After finding them and settling into her home office, she logs in to her e-mail and sees a message from Sandy about the time of their reservation for dinner. Her memory clicks in. She calls her other friend to reschedule so she can keep her promise to Sandy. She would never want to make Sandy sad or hurt her feelings.

Using her intuition, Marnie begins to write newsletter copy. Among her responsibilities are writing a newsletter for internal use to keep the company team connected and writing another newsletter for the public to announce new items. She has music playing in the background and dances in her chair at the keyboard.

The employee newsletter she writes is full of personal stories and human-interest items. Marnie loves doing the interviews for them and collecting information from her coworkers, who are also her friends. This keeps her feeling close to everyone in the company. After finishing the employee newsletter, she turns to the public newsletter, which is designed to be both a clever and innovative informational piece that makes their customers feel involved, cared for, and welcome.

Working from home has been a challenge for Marnie because she loves seeing everyone in person. But she manages to make it work for both her and her employer.

Back at Sandy's home, the research data report is finished. With great satisfaction, Sandy draws a line through it on her whiteboard list. She begins to work on the next project listed on her board and notes what she can complete before leaving to meet Marnie for dinner. Feeling good about her progress, she digs back into her work, the sound of her keyboard the only thing punctuating the silence around her.

Both women are good at their jobs and have formed a solid friendship with one another. They board their horses at the same facility, which has increased the time they can spend with one another. Marnie feels she may not have gotten to know Sandy if they had not had the horse time together. She even suggested that they rent a place together, but Sandy loves living alone and having everything orderly and just so. They meet for dinner whenever they can.

Sandy brings a novel with her to read at the table. She enjoys going a bit early and having a glass of wine. She settles in while waiting for Marnie, who is almost always running late.

Do you see yourself or someone you know in these two people?

. . . .

Everyone is unique and uniquely moves through the world. Being different from others isn't wrong, it's just different.

. . . .

CHAPTER TWO

Root of Temperament

OUR FRIENDSHIPS AND RELATIONSHIPS ARE OFTEN MADE WITH PEOPLE WHO ARE very different from us. As a psychotherapist, I have always had a strong interest in how these differences flavor our lives. But what causes the unique differences in the first place?

Certainly, there are many social factors originating from the region or area in which people are raised. Some children grow up on a farm while others move around a lot with a parent in the military. Some live in a city apartment; others live in a suburban home. Those raising the child also have an impact. Some children have single parents or are with their grandparents; others have both parents as the main influencers. One person may have been raised by strict parents while another may have had permissive or even neglectful parents.

Cultural and religious factors can play a significant part in creating the norms of behavior and interaction. Each culture has its own rituals, styles of parenting, and social expectations. Even gender roles can influence how people express themselves.

Traumatic events during developmental stages, such as the loss of a parent during childhood or some form of abuse, will also shape our reactions and responses to the world. As adults, traumatic events such as battle experiences or spousal abuse can shut a person's more natural preferences down for a while. The person has not changed but their way of responding to the world has been modulated.

Birth order is also a factor. Experts who have studied birth order tell us that an only child does not have a chance to learn how to share or how to argue without siblings to practice on. A middle child may feel unseen but also has more freedom in their position. The baby of a large family can fail to feel the need to do things for themselves since someone has always taken care of things for them. Each of these scenarios will influence behavior and affect how an individual operates in the world. However, it is their "type" that forms the platform on which they build how they will interact through it all—their learning style, the decision style they prefer, and even how they organize their experiences.

Beneath the usual factors sociologists use to view humanity, even more salient factors can be found that establish attraction in friendships and loving marital bonds. These factors are important to understand before we make a commitment, but unfortunately, they are often less understood or even considered when we are forming these committed relationships.

One such factor is our core values. A person's core values are central to who they are. Almost like a computer's operating system, they govern our decisions and determine what feels important. Our values subconsciously dictate our thoughts when we are making decisions in life—not just the large and important thought-filled decisions, but also the daily and seemingly insignificant ones. It is the multitude of these smaller decisions that shape our reality because they combine over time. It is the myriad of smaller decisions—those more spontaneous than thought out and more subconscious

- -

Social, cultural, and religious factors *influence* who we are.

Our core values are *central* to who we are.

Temperament is the *foundation* upon which our values are built.

- -

than conscious—that can add up to extra pounds on the body or a depleted savings account.

There are many theories about how and why we form our values. Many of the factors previously discussed are thought to contribute to their formation, but can we peer even deeper? Could the secret to our core values lie in our temperament?

Horses see what is there.
We see what we think is there.

CHAPTER THREE

A New Looking Glass

WHEN I WAS FINISHING MY MASTER'S DEGREE AT ARIZONA STATE, A FRIEND introduced me to a certification class on using the temperament sorter developed by David Keirsey and Marilyn Bates. I was drawn to its simplicity and ease of use, as well as its accuracy.

Keirsey and Bates were not the first to look at temperament. Hippocrates lectured that there were four major groupings people were "subject to in their way of being": choleric, phlegmatic, melancholic, and sanguine.

In the early 1900s, psychologist Carl Jung contributed the notion of grouping by temperament to the growing field of psychology. Carl Jung and Sigmund Freud were colleagues, but their thinking was different in several basic areas, among them the nature and role of instincts. While Freud saw the libido as the driving instinct for humans, Jung believed that one instinct was no more important than another. He saw people as being different in fundamental ways, even though everyone has the same

> **Understanding different personality types is a gift. Just as wings are a gift that allows birds to soar in the sky, your understanding of the different personality types is a gift that will allow you to soar in your relationships.**

basic instincts. Jung believed that there are differences among people based on each person's individual preferences—those things that are characteristic of them and upon which each person creates their values and lives.

After Jung first developed his approach, the field of psychology began flowing with theories and rich debate. Temperament was forgotten as psychologists formed two distinct camps based on two distinct theories: the behaviorist theory and the dynamics theory. These two camps gave explanations that were based on unconscious motives, seeded in past experiences, or a mixture of both. For a few decades, the views of Jung and Hippocrates were set aside and forgotten.

In the 1940s and 1950s, Isabel Myers and her mother, Kathryn Briggs, reacquainted themselves and the world with the early works of Carl Jung. Through research, they developed and tested the Myers-Briggs Type Indicator (MBTI), which they published in 1962. Isabel Myers and Kathryn Briggs identified four distinct preferential differences between people in how they live in the world, take in information, make decisions, and structure the world. These they described as extroversion/introversion (E/I), sensing/intuition (S/N), thinking/feeling (T/F), and judging/perceiving (J/P). The possible combination of choices netted sixteen personality types: ESTP, ESFP, ENFP, ENTP, ESTJ, ESFJ, ENTJ, ENFJ, ISTJ, ISFJ, INTJ, ISTP, ISFP, INFP, INFJ, INTP. The MBTI began to be used worldwide. In many settings, the MBTI is considered the gold standard for the field of typology, and the instrument is still used widely by psychologists and other professionals. Additionally, many people have taken the MBTI in college or corporate settings.

In the 1940s, David Keirsey (1921–2013) also began researching human behavior, and from that research, he developed the Keirsey Temperament Theory. In 1978, he presented his theory with coauthor Marilyn Bates in the book *Please Understand Me*. In that book, he introduced the Keirsey Temperament Sorter (KTS).

The KTS is an adaptation of the MBTI, and the two instruments are similar in both results and statistical significance. But the KTS is quicker to take and can be administered by laypersons. For these reasons, it is used widely in schools, human resource departments, and churches, as well as on dating websites. It is also used by therapists of all disciplines.

I studied with David Kiersey and began using his sorter in my practice. It is the KTS that is the basis for this book.

Although not yet demonstrated by the scientists who study DNA, it is commonly thought in the typology community that we bring our preferences (temperament) into the world when we are born and that these preferences give rise to our type. I have come to think of it as being similar to a baby being predisposed to being a right-handed person or a left-handed person. There is no right or wrong. It is a preference dialed into us at a basic level.

Our temperament leads to the formation of our essential values as much as any other factor. And our values, which subconsciously drive our decisions, create our reality, which ultimately forms our destiny. What could be more important to understand about yourself? Temperament governs our perceptions and preferences throughout our lives. This is not something in need of changing in any way. There is no correct or superior temperament. But by raising our awareness of our own temperament, we can better understand our behavior, especially in relationships with others who we befriend, marry, parent, or work with. Differences in temperament are strong contributing factors in the development of highly different personalities in siblings who have had very similar experiences, and these differences may be evident even when the siblings are quite small.

When looking at temperament as it gives expression in type, it is important to understand that type does not change. The essence or center of a person's type remains the same throughout life. We may soften as we mature and age, and sometimes situations demand that we adapt. For instance, a person may get a job that requires them to be on time and highly organized. If that person is not wired to be on time and highly organized, they can still develop those skills in order to be successful at their job. It will probably never feel easy, but with enough motivation, they can develop those skills, just as a right-handed person who has seriously injured their right hand can adapt and learn to use their left hand for things previously done with their right hand. But they will still be a right-handed person. In the same way, a person may adapt out of necessity, and that adaptation may appear to change their temperament and type, but they will still fundamentally hold the temperament and type they brought with them into the world.

I have used the Keirsey Temperament Sorter (KTS) for over thirty years and find it to be much easier and quicker for clients to take than the MBTI. There are fewer questions used to type the person, and it takes most people only about twenty minutes to take the test. And after studying and working with the instrument in depth for so long, I have developed an ear for it. Without testing a person, I can hear the client's type expressed in the choice of words they use in their everyday speech and I can observe the traits in their actions.

Awareness is the key to healing, and a great deal of understanding about the framework of an individual's personality is revealed through knowing and understanding their type. A person's daily habits, strengths, and even pet peeves can all be seen within the framework of type. And when we understand and appreciate the differences between types, we develop very deep levels of compassion for both ourselves and others. Even a cursory understanding can make a huge difference, but if you are a person who really is intrigued to dig into this area of study, I encourage you to start by reading *Please Understand Me* by David Keirsey and Marilyn Bates.

After Keirsey and Bates created their sorter, other sorters were birthed and hit the market with all types of paradigms from colors to discs to animals, each with its own set of parameters. I have delved into most of them, and in my experience, they pale by comparison to the KTS—which is closely tied to the original sorter, the MBTI—for the purpose of understanding temperament.

Over the years, I have deepened my own thoughts and ideas about typology and will be applying those along with Keirsey's work throughout this book. As we gain clarity of understanding about ourselves and what makes us unique, we also start to accept and comprehend others. Naturally, along with understanding those around us, we begin to appreciate how they are different from us. Instead of working to change others we build stronger relationships through acceptance, which leads to a healthier, happier coexistence.

Don't set yourself up to make your journey difficult. Do it with joy and ease.

Melisa's Trail

After having horses all my life, I began experimenting with my horses in relation to my therapy clients in the early 1980s. There was no internet to surf at that point so I had no way of going online to see if anyone else was bringing their horses and therapy clients together as I was. Of course, even though I was unaware of it, Barb Rector and others were also tapping into the collective consciousness of the universe. They were out there. I just didn't know about them. I had no one to follow so I trusted myself to develop and refine my own method.

I was a therapist in private practice with a certification in Gestalt therapy. In 1986, I founded my company, Touched by a Horse, Inc.®, and developed a successful private practice with individual clients, couples, and families. I also led corporate workshops and luxury retreats. Along with this work, I also trained and showed horses and established a successful boarding and training ranch in Arizona.

Then, in 1998, I moved from Arizona to Colorado and reestablished my ranch in a new location. This involved moving forty-five head of our top horses and still operating

- -

**Communication is driven by our type
preferences.**

- -

our Arizona location with sixty-five boarders and two trainers. I continued as a Gestalt therapist with a thriving private practice. I had also fallen in love with the coaching model and had become a successful business coach. At the same time, I continued to develop my equine Gestalt model and trademarked it as the Equine Gestalt Coaching Method® (ECGMethod®). With managing both ranches, showing horses, and being a mom, I was busy, so coaching and doing therapy retreats with my EGCMethod® fit perfectly into our life. I also trained other coaches in coaching methods for a national business coaching company and, once again, the Keirsey Temperament Sorter came into play as a useful and enlightening tool. I taught it through webinars and classes as a tool for coaches to gain quick insight they could use to benefit their clientele.

By 2008, I had been a clinician on the equine expo circuit for several years, and the demand to learn my unusual healing method through horses had grown. I decided to offer a certification program for training others in my Equine Gestalt Coaching Method®.

When I opened the Touched by a Horse Certification Program in 2008, I made the decision to offer my program not only to therapists, but also to coaches. I knew that there were other programs being offered, but I also knew that clients could accomplish deep healing with my method and I suspected that my program was unique. Surely there was room for multiple models in what appeared to be a growing field.

In order to learn my method, the students needed to be exposed to and master a wide variety of psychological and human dynamic curricula. And to be fully competent, I knew that the students would need to begin by knowing a great deal about themselves.

One of the key instruments I decided to use was the KTS, which my certification program students learned so deeply that they could usually determine type without even using the test.

Today, I have certified practitioners in the Equine Gestalt Coaching Method® all over the US and Canada, and their ranks are growing globally. These coaches are well trained as Gestaltists and have, as their coach partners, horses whose energy fields and behavior they can read to help guide the work. The coaches have a deep knowledge of both human and equine somatic energy fields, loads of coaching tools and techniques, and a robust understanding of human dynamics with a strong experiential understanding in typology.

Carolyn Fitzpatrick, my coauthor, is a Certified EGCM Coach with a successful practice at her beautiful farm in Amherst, Virginia. Her farm is the location of our East Coast trainings. As Carolyn was going through the two years of training in the program, she discovered that she loved the training on the KTS. One day, remembering an aside I made at a clinic about a horse's temperament, she asked for more explanation and later encouraged me to write this book. Carolyn has been a professional breeder and trainer of horses for many years and found the typology research and process both useful and fascinating. Her instincts told her others would also find the process, as applied to both humans and horses, useful, interesting, and fun.

Since this application of the KTS to horses and the horse-human relationship had never before been presented, we collaborated on the project with David Keirsey's blessing. It is a fascinating journey that is certain to bring forth new thought and fun discussion as you begin to view your equine partners in a new way.

Perhaps a smart place to start is for you to take the KTS, which will help you learn about your own preferences.

Later in the book, you will apply the Equusology Sorter to one of your own horses. Not only will that process further your understanding of your horse, but it will also promote a better sense of how the two of you relate to one another.

Knowing the preferences of others in your life and embracing the differences between them and you builds better relationships.

Taking Your Keirsey Temperament Sorter

BEFORE WE DISCUSS THE KEIRSEY TEMPERAMENT SORTER, LET'S HAVE YOU TAKE IT to discover who *you* are. Before you start, here are some key points and a little guidance.

1. Find a quiet place where you will not be disturbed by a child, your boss, a cell phone call, or other interruptions. It takes the average person about twenty minutes to complete the questionnaire.

2. Take a quick look at the answer sheet. You will be making a check mark in box "a" or "b" for each question. Notice that the answers run from left to right, not down the page in columnar form, so the answer to question 2 will be on the same row as the answer to question 1, not below it.

3. Do *not* ask anyone else what the question means. After all, someone else's understanding of the question would reflect their own view of the world—and their own type—not yours.

4. Answer *all* the questions as you go through the test without skipping any of them.

5. It is important to answer each question honestly from the standpoint of who you truly are, not as you think or feel it "should" be answered or how you believe a boss or a mate would like you to answer it. This is about you and who you truly are. There are no right or wrong answers, just answers that reflect who you are.

6. Give the answer that fits who you are *most* of the time, not under specific situations.

NOTE: Multiple copies of the score sheet have been provided for your use.

◉ THE KEIRSEY TEMPERAMENT SORTER

1. At a party do you
   a. interact with many, including strangers
   b. interact with a few, known to you

2. Are you more
   a. realistic
   b. philosophically inclined

3. Are you more intrigued by
   a. facts
   b. similes

4. Are you usually more
   a. fair minded
   b. kind hearted

5. Do you tend to be more
   a. dispassionate
   b. sympathetic

6. Do you prefer to work
   a. to deadlines
   b. just "whenever"

7. Do you tend to choose
   a. rather carefully
   b. somewhat impulsively

8. At parties do you
   a. stay late, with increasing energy
   b. leave early, with decreased energy

9. Are you a more
    a. sensible person
    b. reflective person

10. Are you more drawn to
    a. hard data
    b. abstruse ideas

11. Is it more natural for you to be
    a. fair to others
    b. nice to others

12. In first approaching others are you more
    a. impersonal and detached
    b. personal and engaging

13. Are you usually more
    a. punctual
    b. leisurely

14. Does it bother you more having things
    a. incomplete
    b. completed

15. In your social groups do you
    a. keep abreast of others' happenings
    b. get behind on the news

16. Are you usually more interested in
    a. specifics
    b. concepts

17. Do you prefer writers who
    a. say what they mean
    b. use lots of analogies

18. Are you more naturally
    a. impartial
    b. compassionate

19. In judging are you more likely to be
    a. impersonal
    b. sentimental

20. Do you usually
    a. settle things
    b. keep options open

21. Are you usually rather
    a. quick to agree to a time
    b. reluctant to agree to a time

22. In phoning do you
    a. just start talking
    b. rehearse what you'll say

23. Facts
    a. speak for themselves
    b. usually require interpretation

24. Do you prefer to work with
    a. practical information
    b. abstract ideas

25. Are you inclined to be more
  a. cool headed
  b. warm hearted

26. Would you rather be
  a. more just than merciful
  b. more merciful than just

27. Are you more comfortable
  a. setting a schedule
  b. putting things off

28. Are you more comfortable with
  a. written agreements
  b. handshake agreements

29. In company do you
  a. start conversations
  b. wait to be approached

30. Traditional common sense is
  a. usually trustworthy
  b. often misleading

31. Children often do not
  a. make themselves useful enough
  b. daydream enough

32. Are you usually more
  a. tough minded
  b. tender hearted

33. Are you more
  a. firm than gentle
  b. gentle than firm

34. Are you more prone to keep things
  a. well organized
  b. open-ended

35. Do you put more value on the
  a. definite
  b. variable

36. Does new interaction with others
  a. stimulate and energize you
  b. tax your reserves

37. Are you more frequently
  a. a practical sort of person
  b. an abstract sort of person

38. Which are you drawn to
  a. accurate perception
  b. concept information

39. Which is more satisfying
  a. to discuss an issue thoroughly
  b. to arrive at agreement on an issue

40. Which rules you more
  a. your head
  b. your heart

41. Are you more comfortable with work
    a. contracted
    b. done on a casual basis

42. Do you prefer things to be
    a. neat and orderly
    b. optional

43. Do you prefer
    a. many friends with brief contact
    b. a few friends with longer contact

44. Are you more drawn to
    a. substantial information
    b. credible assumptions

45. Are you more interested in
    a. production
    b. research

46. Are you more comfortable when you are
    a. objective
    b. personal

47. Do you value in yourself more that you are
    a. unwavering
    b. devoted

48. Are you more comfortable with
    a. final statements
    b. tentative statements

49. Are you more comfortable
    a. after a decision
    b. before a decision

50. Do you
    a. speak easily and at length with strangers
    b. find little to say to strangers

51. Are you usually more interested in the
    a. particular instance
    b. general case

52. Do you feel
    a. more practical than ingenious
    b. more ingenious than practical

53. Are you typically more a person of
    a. clear reason
    b. strong feeling

54. Are you inclined more to be
    a. fair-minded
    b. sympathetic

55. Is it preferable mostly to
   a. make sure things are arranged
   b. just let things happen

56. Is it your way more to
   a. get things settled
   b. put off settlement

57. When the phone rings do you
   a. hasten to get to it first
   b. hope someone else will answer

58. Do you prize more in yourself a
   a. good sense of reality
   b. good imagination

59. Are you drawn more to
   a. fundamentals
   b. overtones

60. In judging are you usually more
   a. neutral
   b. charitable

61. Do you consider yourself more
   a. clear headed
   b. good willed

62. Are you more prone to
   a. schedule events
   b. take things as they come

63. Are you a person that is more
   a. routinized
   b. whimsical

64. Are you more inclined to be
   a. easy to approach
   b. somewhat reserved

65. Do you have more fun with
   a. hands-on-experience
   b. blue-sky fantasy

66. In writings do you prefer
   a. the more literal
   b. the more figurative

67. Are you usually more
   a. unbiased
   b. compassionate

68. Are you typically more
   a. just than lenient
   b. lenient than just

69. Is it more like you to
   a. make snap judgments
   b. delay making judgments

70. Do you tend to be more
   a. deliberate than spontaneous
   b. spontaneous than deliberate

THE KEIRSEY TEMPERAMENT SORTER SCORE SHEET

	a	b		a	b		a	b		a	b		a	b		a	b		a	b
1			2			3			4			5			6			7		
8			9			10			11			12			13			14		
15			16			17			18			19			20			21		
22			23			24			25			26			27			28		
29			30			31			32			33			34			35		
36			37			38			39			40			41			42		
43			44			45			46			47			48			49		
50			51			52			53			54			55			56		
57			58			59			60			61			62			63		
64			65			66			67			68			69			70		

1 [   ] [   ] 2   3 [   ] [   ] 4   5 [   ] [   ] 6   7 [   ] [   ] 8

   E   I   S   N   T   F   J   P

THE KEIRSEY TEMPERAMENT SORTER SCORE SHEET

	a	b		a	b		a	b		a	b		a	b		a	b		a	b
1			2			3			4			5			6			7		
8			9			10			11			12			13			14		
15			16			17			18			19			20			21		
22			23			24			25			26			27			28		
29			30			31			32			33			34			35		
36			37			38			39			40			41			42		
43			44			45			46			47			48			49		
50			51			52			53			54			55			56		
57			58			59			60			61			62			63		
64			65			66			67			68			69			70		

1 ___ ___ 2   3 ___ ___ 4   5 ___ ___ 6   7 ___ ___ 8

E   I   **S   N**   **T   F**   **J   P**

THE KEIRSEY TEMPERAMENT SORTER SCORE SHEET

	a	b		a	b		a	b		a	b		a	b		a	b		a	b
1			2			3			4			5			6			7		
8			9			10			11			12			13			14		
15			16			17			18			19			20			21		
22			23			24			25			26			27			28		
29			30			31			32			33			34			35		
36			37			38			39			40			41			42		
43			44			45			46			47			48			49		
50			51			52			53			54			55			56		
57			58			59			60			61			62			63		
64			65			66			67			68			69			70		

1			2		3			4		5			6		7			8
	E	**I**				**S**	**N**				**T**	**F**				**J**	**P**	

THE KEIRSEY TEMPERAMENT SORTER SCORE SHEET

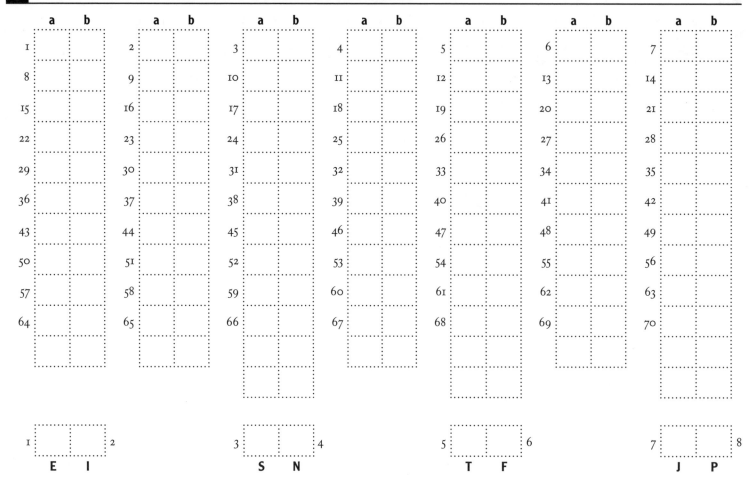

	a	b		a	b		a	b		a	b		a	b		a	b		a	b
1			2			3			4			5			6			7		
8			9			10			11			12			13			14		
15			16			17			18			19			20			21		
22			23			24			25			26			27			28		
29			30			31			32			33			34			35		
36			37			38			39			40			41			42		
43			44			45			46			47			48			49		
50			51			52			53			54			55			56		
57			58			59			60			61			62			63		
64			65			66			67			68			69			70		

1			2		3			4		5			6		7			8
E		**I**			**S**		**N**			**T**		**F**			**J**		**P**

◗ THE KEIRSEY TEMPERAMENT SORTER SCORE SHEET

	a	b		a	b		a	b		a	b		a	b		a	b		a	b
1			2			3			4			5			6			7		
8			9			10			11			12			13			14		
15			16			17			18			19			20			21		
22			23			24			25			26			27			28		
29			30			31			32			33			34			35		
36			37			38			39			40			41			42		
43			44			45			46			47			48			49		
50			51			52			53			54			55			56		
57			58			59			60			61			62			63		
64			65			66			67			68			69			70		

1   2
E   **I**

3   4
S   **N**

5   6
T   **F**

7   8
J   **P**

◐ DIRECTIONS FOR SCORING

You now have a check in either box "a" or "b" for each question.

1. Notice that the first row of blank boxes near the bottom of the answer sheet is numbered 1–8.

2. Add *down* each row so that the total number of "a" answers is written in the box at the bottom of each "a" column. Do the same for the "b" answers you have checked. Each of the fourteen boxes near the bottom should have a number in it.

3. On your answer sheet, transfer the number in box #1 of the answer sheet to box #1 below (lowest box). Do this for box #2 as well. You now have a total number for the E and the I. The combined number for boxes 1 and 2 should equal 10.

4. As you continue bringing your answers down the columns across this row, notice there are two #3 columns, two #4, etc. Add each column *downward* placing the total number of checks in each column in the corresponding box number.

5. Each of the first set of numbers (i.e. first box #3 and first box #4) will be carried in the lower boxes under the second set of numbers so they can be combined into one total (just as you did for boxes #1 and #2). The two #3 numbers will be added together downward to provide the number placed in the lowest box and the two #4 numbers will be added together downward to provide the number placed in the lowest box. You should now have a total number for the S and the N. The combined numbers for the lowest boxes on the answer sheet should equal 20.

6. Now continue this scoring method, bringing down the total for each column first, transferring the first set of scores for those numbers to the lower boxes so they may be added for one combined total score. This process will provide you with one score

for the T, F, J and P. The combined numbers for #5 and #6 should equal 20 and the combined numbers for #7 and #8 should equal 20.

7. Now you have four pairs of numbers. Circle the letter below that is the larger number of the pair. If the two numbers of any pair are the same, then do not circle either number but put a large "X" below them and circle the "X."

If you have an "**X**" in your type, yours is a mixed type, which means your preferences are nearly the same between those types. This presents other challenges.

Having identified your type, the task now is to read the type description and to decide how well or how poorly the description fits. If you have an "X" in your type, yours is a combination of two types, so you will probably find you have characteristics from each of the descriptions that are applicable for you. For example, if you have an "X" in the J/P category, you may find the "J" description fits you in some situations and the "P" description fits you in other situations. You may prefer closure on some things and like to leave options open in other areas of your life, as we will discuss in Chapter Eight.

Now that you know your type, let's take a look at what it all means. In the next few chapters, you will define your specific preferences and traits. The lens you will begin to peer through will illuminate your unique way of moving in the world. At the same time, you may begin to appreciate the differences between you and those close to you.

. . . .

You have now identified your "type." It should be one of the following.

INFP	ISFP	INTP	ISTP
ENFP	ESFP	ENTP	ESTP
INFJ	ISFJ	INTJ	ISTJ
ENFJ	ESFJ	ENTJ	ESTJ

. . . .

**Percentage of the General Population
Represented by Each Indicator Category**

E: 75%	I: 25%
S: 75%	N: 25%
T: 50%	F: 50%
J: 50%	P: 50%

CHAPTER SIX

Differences Are Preferences

WE ARE ALL DIFFERENT IN A MYRIAD OF WAYS, AND MOST OF THE TIME WE HONOR and celebrate that fact. Our preferences make up who we are as individuals. Using this information and finding your type is not about putting a label on yourself or being placed in a box. It is about raising awareness of your unique preferences.

These preferences should be seen as natural or inherent choices. It is important to understand your natural preferences, but it is also important to build strength in the core skills of the opposite preference. Your innate preferences will come naturally, so focus can be placed on the "weaker" side, just as a trainer works a horse longer to their less dominant side to strengthen him. Developing skills that fit the preference opposite to your own natural one can benefit you in communication, working habits, and other areas of proficiency.

Even after developing these "weaker" or less dominant sides to our temperament, we need to remember these are *skills* we have gained not preferences, and the basic preferences will remain dominant.

Think of a right-handed person who becomes a surgeon. To be a skilled surgeon she develops her left-handedness. Her right-handedness will still be dominant, but she will now have more flexibility and skill, thanks to developing her less dominant hand.

Our selection of words when communicating is often driven by our type preferences, but through awareness, we can adjust our choice of words to create a clearer statement when our words are directed to someone whose type is different from our own. Certain words resonate with meaning and importance keyed to their type preference. For an SJ, the word "integrity" is key, and it will stand out in a discussion with them. If they are having the discussion with an NF and refer to "authentic connection" instead of using the word "integrity," they will be more fully understood by the NF.

As an employer, I take type into consideration when hiring employees. If I am hiring for a person to answer the phone, meet prospective clients, and represent our company in an expo booth, I will select someone who scores as an extravert because they will be comfortable meeting new people and having a diverse work environment. If I am hiring for an administrative assistant, I look for someone whose strengths include paying close attention to details and managing data in an organized fashion.

I also take into account that desk location adjustments may need to be made for that person to increase their performance. If I hire a person who is a strong copywriter and they test as a high introvert, placing their desk in a bullpen will affect their performance negatively. A more socially outgoing person's energy rises if they are in a bullpen or have the office with the most traffic, but the person who is more introverted prefers solitude. Placed in a bullpen or another high-traffic location, they will lose productivity and become quickly fatigued by the forced interactions.

At meetings or in parenting, remembering to allow an introvert to process internally or in writing before demanding their input can promote gains in garnering valuable information. Likewise, when an N is working with or married to an S, if the N

. . . .

Cues

These words and expressions are favorites for each type when expressing themselves and also more noticed by this type when reading or listening to communication from others.

E	**I**	**T**	**F**
Sociability	Territoriality	Objective	Subjective
Interaction	Concentration	Principles	Values
Breadth	Depth	Firmness	Persuasion
Extensive	Intensive	Justice	Mercy
		Measured	Familiar
		Impersonal	Personal

S	**N**	**J**	**P**
Experience	Hunches	Settled	Pending
Past	Future	Closed	Open ended
Actual	Possible	Fixed	Flexible
Sensible	Imaginative	Plan ahead	Adapt as you go
Fact	Fiction	Closure	Open options
Perspiration	Inspiration		

. . . .

remembers that the S seeks out more details to understand what is being said, they can provide those details, thereby creating a bridge to better clarity.

In a marriage, how each partner prefers to share the weekend block of time can be quite different. One may want to get chores completed on Saturday and relax on Sunday afternoon after the to-do list is done while the other may exclaim that they have been working all week and want to rest or play on Saturday, then get a few chores done Sunday . . . maybe.

An ENFJ wife who waits, wishing her ISTJ husband will say something loving to her, can learn to appreciate and make note of the ISTJ's many actions that show love rather than express it in words.

Just as our human relationships are impacted by type, so are our relationships with our horses, where communication and connection is also important. One horse may need the corner aisle way stall where he can see everything happening in the facility while another may want the end stall, which is buffered by the tack room and provides little contact or interaction with other horses.

Differences abound and we can practice acceptance of self and others by not making them right or wrong. This is never about "fixing" another person or even "fixing" a trait or characteristic within ourselves. It is about understanding and gaining insight into how the different preferences serve each person.

In the twentieth century, the belief that we are all fundamentally the same was a strong notion that was reflected in our political systems and government institutions. Our schools, hospitals, and other organizations were designed to fit everyone. David Keirsey pointed out that democracy had inadvertently inspired the notion that because we are all equal, we are all alike. Of course, this is not true.

As I stated earlier, a person's type is as innate as whether they are right-handed or left-handed. It is our natural state. It is our truth in the seat of our personality and our

. . . .

There is no right type and no wrong type.
Horses have preferences, too.

. . . .

being. It becomes the platform upon which our governing core values and many of our perceptions in life are formed.

A true appreciation of self and others for our differences can be refreshing. You can begin to look at your friends, your spouse, or your boss with a new perspective that allows for understanding instead of hoping they will change. You will note that every type has its own set of strengths. And you will come to understand that what you have seen as odd traits or traits that do not serve them may actually be serving them well. There are no right or wrong preferences in type.

Carl Jung knew that the degree to which a trait was expressed was of material importance. A person who scores a 13-J and one who scores a 19-J will vary greatly in the degree of their preference strength. The 13-J has 7 points on the P side of the fence. They would be very organized on things that really matter to them but not as organized on the things that do not matter as much. Maybe their tack room is clean and organized but their car trunk is a mess. They would be on time or early for things that matter, such as their job, but resistant to making personal appointments with rigid times. If you schedule something more social than business with them at their ranch, they may say, "Great! Let's meet at the barn around 1:00," allowing their P side to express itself by going with the flow.

The person who scored 19-J is in direct contrast to that experience. Often, the 19 or 20 is a perfectionist with a hard inner critic who is filled with high expectations for their own performance and environment. They arrive early everywhere, taking with them a productive tool such as a book to read or something to work on to avoid becoming stressed while waiting. Their living environment and personal work space must be efficiently organized or they cannot focus enough to work or even enjoy their work.

When reviewing your scores, remember that the higher the score, the more true to the type you will see in the traits. Those whose scores are more evenly split—for instance, a

10-J and 10-P—can be considered ambidextrous in that they have a lot of flexibility in using some traits from both sides. However, without a dominant preference for J or P, they may confuse others a bit. For instance, a person evenly split between J and P may have a very clean and organized tack room while having a clothes closet that is a total mess. They may have a nicely organized scheduling function on their cell phone but forget to look at it or bring it with them and, therefore, miss appointments.

In the Touched by a Horse certification program, I use the kaleidoscope as a metaphor for the complexity of the human personality. We are each a synergy of all the parts of our personality. Kaleidoscopes are comprised of a finite number of composite pieces, but when you look through a kaleidoscope, the design changes, over and over, as you turn it. In the same way, each of us has many composite pieces to our "self" or personality, and in any given situation, the pieces form a pattern that suits that situation or set of events.

We work on a model of discovering our personal mandala, the composite drawing of our central parts that are operating all the time but in differing order of strengths. You may be aware that you have a strong part of your personality that you could dub as "firm" and yet, if fully explored, there is another true part of you that is "persuadable." "Firm" and "persuadable" may seem to be opposite characteristics, but as they express themselves in the kaleidoscope of who you are, they each play a role. You may be firm in your job as a corporate manager but persuadable when you are with your husband. We all have hundreds of operating parts.

Your born temperament and type are the keys to your personal mandala, while your past experiences, your birth order, and your culture also play a part as the myriad components comprising who you are fall into place within the kaleidoscope of your ongoing life. The components of your type have guided you to whether you sit in the front row in class (E) or prefer the back row (I), whether you love math and science (S)

> **The higher the score, the stronger the preference.**

or prefer language arts (N). It impacts whether you are drawn to drama movies and plays (NF), enjoy scientific documentaries (T), or would rather hike on an unknown trail (SP). The J type keeps their files in alphabetical order and everything in a file. This may be efficient for them as a J, but it would never work for a P. The P has a box or a pile where all papers are thrown, and rather than taking the time to organize files, they would rather search through the box if they need to find something.

As we mature in life, our basic type stays the same, but it can strengthen or lessen.

And with maturity, we also learn to adapt to others and their preferences to make life run more smoothly at home or at work. For example, if it is very important to a spouse to have the bedroom floor clear of shoes and clothes because they are a high J, a P spouse who is less in need of the orderliness may comply in order to please their J spouse and keep peace at home. But when the J spouse is out of town, the P mate may revert to a more relaxed state, including leaving shoes and clothes where they fall when removed and picking them up before their spouse returns.

At fifty, when we may be more at peace with ourselves than we were when we were younger, it may be less important to us to make our preferences known than it was at thirty. Although our type remains the same, we develop the ability to be more flexible and adapt to working and living with others as we mature.

And, as pointed out earlier, those who have scores evenly split within a category may find that different situations trigger which preference in a pair (E or I, S or N, T or F, J or P) is activated. If this is true for you, consider whether the parts of yourself you consider to be "at odds" might actually be expressing the very nature of your preferences as a person who has evenly split preferences within a preference pair category. If so, you will now understand why.

There is much to take into consideration with type, but as you become more familiar with yourself and apply your type to how you behave in life, you will begin to understand the broad scope of influence your specific type score has in governing your decisions and shaping your reality. A fuller understanding of the score values and how they relate to the other preferences unfolds like a roadmap before you.

. . . .

EXAMPLE: An invitation arrives for a party to be held in a month. If you are 5-E and 5-I, your extraverted half happily responds that you will come. You are looking forward to seeing all the people who you know will be attending. Hurray! But on the day of the party you have a deep sense of dread and would give anything to be curling up on your sofa with a good book. You really don't want to go the party. Your introverted half is awakened now.

. . . .

CHAPTER SEVEN

The Preference Pairs

LET'S TAKE A LOOK AT THE FOUR MAJOR CHOICE POINTS OF DIFFERENCE, THE "preference pairs" E/I, S/N, T/F, and J/P. These are represented in the columns on the answer sheet.

⬤ THE KEIRSEY TEMPERAMENT SORTER SCORE SHEET

	a	b		a	b		a	b		a	b		a	b		a	b		a	b
1			2			3			4			5			6			7		
8			9			10			11			12			13			14		
15			16			17			18			19			20			21		
22			23			24			25			26			27			28		
29			30			31			32			33			34			35		
36			37			38			39			40			41			42		
43			44			45			46			47			48			49		
50			51			52			53			54			55			56		
57			58			59			60			61			62			63		
64			65			66			67			68			69			70		

1 ▢ ▢ 2   3 ▢ ▢ 4   5 ▢ ▢ 6   7 ▢ ▢ 8

   E   I   **S   N**   **T   F**   **J   P**

The first column on the score sheet indicates Extraversion (E) or Introversion (I), which is your orientation to the world around you and how you prefer to express yourself, as well as engage with others.

The second column indicates Sensing (S) or Intuition (N), which relates to your learning styles and preferences for gaining information from the world around you. The third column provides information on your preference for Thinking (T) and Feeling (F), which indicates whether you are more likely to make decisions from the head or the heart. The last column, the one farthest to the right, represents a preference for either Judging (J) or Perceiving (P), which indicates how you prefer to organize and relate to time, and space, and your environment.

◉ EXTRAVERSION (E) AND INTROVERSION (I)

This is the most commonly known, understood, and used temperament pairing in our American vocabulary. This pairing represents a person's social energy. A person who is more extraverted (E) will find their juices flowing when there is social interaction. Talking, playing, and interacting raises their energy level. By contrast, an introvert (I) requires solitude to recover or refill their energy banks

In my practice, I began to see it also as a difference in distilling thought. The E needs to process orally with another person. For the high E, this is a must. This action of speaking out loud helps the E distill their thoughts to a simpler declaration. This means that some of what they are saying cannot be taken as fact. It is only after this process that they come to their bottom line.

Here is a story that may help.

A large Texas ranch owner went out to check on one hundred tons of baled alfalfa that his men were moving into the hay barns for winter storage. All the barns also

Note: The E/I column totals 10 rather than 20 like the other three do. You can multiply by 2 to get the equivalent of the strength of your number if you would like to. A 7/3 would then be a 14/6, which may illustrate more clearly the relative difference.

75% of the general population is E (extravert) and only 25% is I (introvert).

had equipment stored in them. As he rode up, his foreman waved, and he could see the ranch hands moving bale after bale by hand in the summer sun. They were about halfway through the task.

"Looks like you have been making progress," the rancher said to his foreman. "It would have been better if we had moved all the tractor equipment into that south barn and put all this hay in the two north ones. That would have made it easier for the crew to work on the equipment during inclement weather." He went on to talk about what tractors needed what repairs, what was being prepared for lunch, and even what new piece of machinery he was thinking of purchasing. When his cell phone rang, he waved and rode off.

Wanting to make the rancher happy, the foreman stopped the hands in their work and told them they were going to reorganize and move all the equipment to the south barn and all the hay to the two north sheds. The men groaned and began moving the heavy hay.

The next evening, the ranch owner rode over expecting to see the job complete and was taken aback by the fact that it was not. "I thought y'all would be finished here by now," he said.

"I did what you asked and reorganized the sheds," the foreman replied.

The rancher slowly shook his head and smiled. "Happens all the time to me. I never said I wanted you to *do* all that, I was just thinking out loud."

A person with a higher E score (8 or higher) often has an experience like the rancher. Someone will say, "But you said . . ." and the extravert will reply, "No, I never said that."

The extravert was simply thinking out loud in a process of discovering what it was they wanted to express. This is the way they distill their thoughts, but it can lead to confusion or even frustration for others. The extravert is just trying to sort things out and come to some clarity, but the lack of filtering in their communication can make it difficult for others to know what they are actually saying and what they want. If others know that the person is an extravert in the process of distilling information, then the communication between them may be easier and more fruitful. And those communicating with the extravert may realize that they sometimes need to ask for clarification.

By contrast, the introvert needs time to process, preferably without interruption or distraction. They may appear withdrawn, shy, or even snobby to the extravert when they actually just require time to be able to think and process what they want to express. If pressured to respond before they have the time and space to process, they may withhold valuable input or ideas that they have not distilled at that point. When the introvert is distilling their thoughts, an extravert may think that nothing is happening because the distilling is happening within the introvert instead of verbally, as the extravert does it. In actuality, a great deal is happening that the extravert is simply not privy to.

In a group situation, the introvert is more comfortable when they have a chance to prepare ahead and are certain of their role. They are often excellent observers and listeners and will position themselves for those activities, but they are less likely to speak spontaneously or contribute to a group discussion. Instead, they quietly distill what they are taking in and when required to make a statement, it will reflect their bottom line.

Let's look at another scenario. If you were giving a surprise birthday party for a dear friend and you wanted to make sure it would please them, it would be very helpful to look at their type. Are they an extravert or an introvert? How would that impact the party you plan?

. . . .

**I'm feeling pretty alone. I wish I had
  company. (E)**
The more, the merrier. (E)
I need my space. (I)
Nobody listens to me. (I)

. . . .

The extravert would appreciate a surprise birthday party with both friends they haven't seen in many years and current friends. You might even throw in a few people you want them to meet because you know they will enjoy them. You plan for lots of music, a variety of food, and even a PowerPoint of pictures from their childhood that will be set to music. You know that the evening will run into the early hours of the morning with everyone laughing and talking. The party's overall theme would be "the more the merrier."

What about an introvert? How would you plan for their ideal surprise party? You would take the time to find out what their favorite nice restaurant is. You would research where your friend likes to sit in that restaurant and might discover that she prefers sitting by a window that is away from the crowd instead of one that looks out at the nearby water but is in a busier part of the restaurant. You invite the introvert's best friend or spouse. If she is married, you invite the couple she and her spouse are closest to. Then you make reservations for this small, intimate group. At the table, you leave a beautiful handwritten note that says you want them to relax, take their time, and enjoy the meal, which is on you. You know that the introvert will get into an in-depth conversation with her small group.

The extravert usually sees the breadth or totality of the event or situation while the introvert likes to see the depth of it. The extravert likes to meet new people, networks easily, and can be very entertaining with their stories. The introvert likes to listen and converse in depth with fewer people, but they really develop their relationships with those people. Both can be valuable styles.

Introverts tend to be territorial. They like to have their own space, a private space. This is how they restore and conserve energy. Extraverts like variety and like having a broader territory in which to navigate. Seeing other people and having social interaction throughout the day charges them.

An introvert can feel quite alone, especially when strangers surround them, while an extravert will easily make a new friend in a crowd of strangers. If that extravert meets that new friend at an airport, she will quickly exchange contact information with them and suggest they get together for dinner the next time they are both in town. But in that same situation, among many people they do not know at an airport, the introvert can feel uncomfortable or even feel deep sadness, particularly if they have not had time to prepare for the experience. This is not to say that introverts don't enjoy engaging with others. They do. They just prefer to find quiet places to engage in a more in-depth discussion.

Return to your own score sheet. The degree to which you are an introvert or an extravert (reflected in how high the score is for each) explains the level to which the preferences will show up. For instance, if someone is an E-6 and an I-4, they will exhibit both some extravert and some introvert preferences, but there will be less strength to the introverted side within them.

Someone with an E-6 and an I-4 might be quite comfortable if they have a role to play such as acting, teaching a class, giving a lecture, or standing in a booth at an expo meeting with thousands of people passing by. However, if they are at an expo and are invited to a meet-and-greet or a social wine and cheese outing, they are likely to pass on that invitation, preferring room service and a night alone to the outing. The E-6 part of them is quite happy interacting with people at the expo booth, but the idea of small talk with a group of strangers pushes their I-4 side to scream.

What if that person is an E-9 and an I-1? They would accept the invitation to the outing, dance, have a good time, and be energized by the fun. Because their strength lies more in the extraverted side of them, extraverted activities will energize them more than introverted activities.

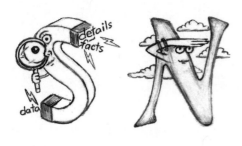

**75% of the general population is
S (sensing) and 25% is N (intuition).**

If only I could touch or smell it. (N)
Life is full of possibilities. (N)
Enough. Break it down in steps. (S)
Don't expose me, teach me. (S)

☾ SENSING (S) AND INTUITION (N)

Sensing (S) and Intuition (N) are the categories that show learning styles—how we learn and take in information. When Keirsey was writing his book thirty years ago, the word "intuition" had not found its way into common daily vocabulary. The meaning has a different connotation when looking at type than it has in general usage. Since the first letter of "introversion" is also an "I," "N" was used as the abbreviation for intuition, just to avoid confusion.

As I have worked with clients using this instrument, I see it as their orientation to the world. The sensing person is interested in *what is*, or reality. Data, facts, and a fact-based methodical approach are preferred by the sensing person. The person for whom intuition is the preference is future oriented and visionary. They see reality as a springboard to possibility. The N person uses metaphor to explain life. The actual present reality holds little interest for the N. It is merely the point on which the unfolding future is built, with all things possible. Complex ideations come "whole" to the N, almost as if they have always known the information. Finding it hard to explain exactly how they know the information, the N focuses on the possibilities that lie ahead. They prize a vivid imagination.

The sensing person (S) is interested in the details and a no-nonsense approach, focusing on specific elements and the facts at hand. They may have hunches but they pay little attention to them or mistrust them. They want to feel down-to-earth, practical, and sensible in their approach to life.

The intuitive person (N) lives in the unfolding gift of what lies ahead and looks forward with anticipation. This can lead to restlessness in some individuals when reality burdens their vision. The N does not view their forward-looking visions as hunches. They are simply pieces of information.

Here is an example of this difference in styles. A new tractor is delivered to a farm, accompanied by a manual in booklet form and a DVD. The manual has a "Please read first" label on it. The S person would take the booklet home that evening and go through it thoroughly. They would also watch the DVD, taking notes on maintenance, fuel types, and other important information provided in the recording. The S person would do both of these things before attempting to drive the tractor, wanting to be clear what step one, step two, and all the remaining steps are to operate and maintain the machine properly.

Conversely, the N person would be eager to drive the tractor and would climb up on the seat to check out how it felt. When looking at the tractor they would see the parts that seem similar to the old tractor—or even their car—and start it up to hear the sound.

Confident that they have the booklet and DVD to look at later for the maintenance charts and fuel types, they put those aside for the time being to experience the tractor firsthand. After the first drive they better understand the quick tips chart that came with the booklet, and they are glad they have the bigger manual if they ever need it to look something up that they cannot intuit.

THINKING (T) AND FEELING (F)

The Thinking (T) and Feeling (F) categories reflect how we make decisions and choices in life.

The thinking (T) person uses their intellect and creates an analysis or forms a strategy. Their choices are based on an impersonal stand. The feeling (F) person reaches their conclusions by drawing on the personal realm and how they feel about the scenario.

For the thinking person (T), things can seem black-and-white. They use logic, research, and principles to make decisions. Policy and procedure is laid out to govern all acts. What matters are fairness and a sense of absolute justice, not personal circumstances. The law or rule is set to serve the greater good. Mercy is bias and therefore not to be entertained. Objective criteria are the means for making choices clear and nonbiased.

The feeling person (F) reaches into their heart and body to discern how they feel about situations when a decision or choice is needed. This does include the mind in that they check to determine if their mind feels calm about a possible choice. But they also check to see if their breathing is deep or shallow, whether their heart feels at ease, and how their gut is processing the choice. For the F, all areas need to be in congruence for the decision to be peacefully made. Feelings about the decision will guide instead of the thinking process the T uses.

The general population is evenly split between thinking (T) and feeling (F) people.

Both types can react emotionally, although the feeling person (F) is likely to make it more visible. While the F can enjoy experiencing a wide range of emotions and even sometimes have little control over exposing them, the T may have an intense emotion that is explored with logic and held within the thinking processes rather than expressed as feeling.

The feeling person resonates with sympathy, compassion, devotion, and extenuating circumstances, and these influence outcomes. The thinking person takes an impersonal stance in analyzing the situation at hand, looking for the rules and boundaries that apply or are related to it.

For example, if you are pulled over for speeding by a police officer who happens to be a T and you tell him your horse is in colic and you have to rush to the barn to meet the vet, he will likely remind you that the law is for everyone and was well thought out to protect everyone, all of the time. Then he will write you a ticket. If, on the other hand, you are pulled over by a police officer who happens to be an F, he will likely see and feel your fear and pain. Instead of writing you a speeding ticket, he may tell you that he is going to let you go with a warning this time. He will remind you to slow down so you can get to that meeting with the vet safely. And as you leave, he might tell you he hopes the best for your horse.

If you ever find yourself pulled over by a police officer while you are hurrying to meet the vet at your barn, hope that the officer is an F!

I'm comfortable in heart space. (F)
But how will she feel about it if I tell her that? (F)
Yes, I'm in my head a lot. (T)
But will she understand what I mean if I tell her that? (T)

🌀 JUDGING (J) AND PERCEIVING (P)

The Judging (J) and Perceiving (P) categories indicate orientation to time, space, and your environment. Once again, the words for the categories—Judging (J) and Perceiving (P)—may not be the words you would automatically associate with time, space, and environment, but some explanation of the two preferences will help.

The judging person (J) has a strong need for organizing both time and space. The J also has a drive for closure, often making a to-do list and feeling euphoria or joy when crossing items off. The high J will wear a watch even though they could check their cell phone for the time. And even if there is as little as five minutes between tasks, they will likely put it to good use. The J creates deadlines and works well to them with a strong push to be finished long beforehand. They have a strong preference for having things orderly, creating organizational systems, and wanting everything in its place.

While the J has a natural work ethic, the P has a play ethic. The perceiving person has a spontaneous way of living and seems to flow through life taking things as they come. They appear less serious than their J counterpart and feel less stress on a daily basis. The P is often more process oriented. They look for ways to make their work fun or enjoyable. In contrast, the J focuses on productivity and has an outcome orientation.

Give the P a deadline and it can be treated as a start date. A high scoring P sees the value in organization and may even buy or set up systems to create it, but the follow-through and maintenance on it is just too much. They prefer to be in the moment with the next urgent thing being what gets taken care of as they go through the day. If they make a to-do list, it is with good intentions, but the list is often lost in the course of getting things done. Time is distorted for the P, and they always believe they can get one more thing done before they need to be somewhere.

· ·

Everything is in its places, just as I like it. (J)

Hurrah, the project is done! Now I can move on to the next thing on my list. (J)

There are so many possibilities. (P)

Let's run. I'll pick things up later. (P)

· ·

Allowing their life to unfold, the perceiving person (P) will take time in their day to play a game of ball with their kids or find a new trail back to the barn. They can be found dreading the finality of a major decision because a better answer might be just around the corner. Completing a purchase causes anxiety because a better buy might become available next week.

The P likes to keep their options open; the J craves and celebrates completion.

Let's use the example of giving a party to explore the differences between a P and a J. The J plans the party weeks in advance. The invitations are sent out with a precise start time and a map to the home. They are mailed to an established guest list with an RSVP. Tasks such as the menu are taken care of well in advance of the party and any items that can be purchased ahead are bought with others ordered for pick up the day before or day of the party. The party theme and any environment enhancements or prepping of tables and chairs are done in advance. If the party is scheduled for a workday, the J will take that day off from work. If it is scheduled for Saturday, the J will likely take Friday off to be certain no detail is left out. The party and its implementation are perfection.

The P has a particularly good day. Some friends are in town visiting, which inspires the idea for a party. The P knows that some people from work are fun to hang out with, as well as a close neighbor or two. Calls are made and e-mails or texts are sent. The P also adds a shout-out in the company break room. "Hey, the party's at my place tonight!" Calls are made on the drive home to order some pizza and a stop for pop and beer is made. As guests arrive, the P is found clearing the newspaper off the sofa, loading the dishwasher with dishes from the previous day's dinner, and getting out some paper plates. The music is already cranking.

Both parties can be fun.

50% of the general population is J (judging) and 50% is P (perceiving).

OH DEAR! I GUESS THREE FILE CABINETS AREN'T GOING TO BE ENOUGH TO STORE ALL MY PLANNING DOCUMENTS FOR THE IMPROMPTU OFFICE PARTY!

YES! THE WHOLE OFFICE WILL BE HERE IN FIVE MINUTES TO PAR-TEE! LEAVES ME PLENTY OF TIME TO CLEAN UP, TAKE A SHOWER AND THROW TOGETHER SOME FOOD!!

THE SIXTEEN POSSIBLE COMBINATIONS OF THE FOUR PREFERENCE PAIRINGS

ESTJ	ISFJ	INFJ	INTJ
ISTP	ISFP	INFP	INTP
ESTP	ESFP	ENFP	ENTP
ESTJ	ESFJ	ENFJ	ENTJ

Once you understand the individual letters in the preference pairs and their indications of preference, you can combine them to form your personal type among the sixteen type combinations. This gives a full picture of you, especially if you take into consideration the level of your score in each section. The higher the score (say 15 or higher for the S/N, T/F, J/P combinations and 7 or more for E/I), the more "true to type" your expression of the traits in that category will be.

To really understand how the combinations show up, however, we need to break it down one more time—this time into four specific groups that reveal the potency of certain combinations that have great predictive value. By knowing a person's type, we can anticipate, rather accurately, what they will say or do most of the time.

The four key combinations are SJ, SP, NF, and NT. Remember, the S/N pairing impacts how we take in information, the T/F pairing impacts how we make decisions, and the J/P pairing impacts how we deal with time, space, and the outside world, in general. These four combinations—SJ, SP, NF, and NT—are particularly powerful in terms of impacting how we see the world, communicate with the world, and act in the world.

With their detail orientation, the S is interested in how to express the facts in an organized fashion and timely manner. Therefore, we always see the S paired with either the J or the P. The pairing with the J allows for an organized flowchart and policy application while the P expresses through creative outlets. The N is less interested in facts than in the larger picture and future movement. Therefore it is paired with the T or the F. When paired with the T, it allows for critique of the possibilities ahead while the F pairing is about connection with others while moving forward.

The S focuses on details, facts, and data. They collect this information and have a need to find a way to organize it in time, space, and their environment before they can rest. If the S is combined with the J, they will be seeking a method to bring structure and a system to the data. They will focus on organizing it in a way that is functional, and they will be dependable in its use. The SJ will create systems of organizing the data so it can be used to form rules or policies that will be of service to others. This is all important to the SJ person because they feel a general sense of responsibility in the world. For instance, a researcher will seek out all the details and create a report that will allow the research to be utilized to improve a policy or claim.

However, when the S is combined with the P, the person is also looking for a way to work with time, space, and their environment. As an S, they have gathered the data and details, but their emphasis is on expressing it with a feeling of flow and freedom. The SP may use creative charts to express the details. They are less interested in the data being useful than in creatively working with the information to start a conversation or a movement. This is often seen in an SP architect who pays close attention to the engineering facts and details of a structure but is also drawn to the artistic expression of beauty within the practicality of the building. The SP may express directly in an art form such as the visual arts, music, or poetry. The need for rules is not present. Instead, the SP needs and is guided by freedom of expression.

When traveling, the J arrives at the airport with enough time to get through security and then have breakfast, do some shopping, and read a novel at the gate.

Their friend the P runs to catch the plane as the doors are closing. The P settles in at her seat with a disheveled look and a super funny story of why she is running late . . . again.

As the chapters ahead unfold, we will lay out each of these four key combinations and go into more detail about them. Grasping this part of the type expressions is central to understanding ourselves and our horses.

Sensing (S): SJ and SP Combinations

ALTHOUGH THERE ARE SIXTEEN POSSIBLE TYPE COMBINATIONS, WE WILL PRIMARILY focus on the major groupings—in this chapter, SJ and SP—with some discussion about how the other preference pair areas may color the field when combined with them. Many of those with a sensing preference seem to have a need to pair that sensing preference with either a preference for judging (J) or perceiving (P).

We know that the S is interested in facts, data, historical perspective, and reality. Whether an S is combined with a T or an F will determine the way in which they express themselves in decision making, but the higher influence is whether the S is combined with the J or the P.

Think of the S person as a data and detail magnet. Layers of specifics and exact dimensions, shades of color, and other details lay at their feet. How will they organize the information? The answer to that is central to whether they are an SJ or an SP.

The SJ wants to tightly organize all the details and data into a systematic approach. This will yield "usable" information. Forming policies and procedures will enable them to use the data and keep everything neatly inside the box in a responsible way. The box serves a greater good, and the SJ will take on responsibility to be of service and to maintain fairness in the distribution or use of the data.

The SP, on the other hand, desires freedom in the way they organize the data. While they also want exact shades of color, dimensions, and other details, they often create their work outside the box. The SP is an artist by nature, displaying the data in a creative manner. They find joy in how they express the details, not in containing, organizing, or finding the utility in them.

For the SP it is the process, not its completion, that draws their interest. The SP is more interested in innovating with the facts than in using a system with the facts. SPs see their contributions as having to do with creating in an open, flowing, evolving way. They do not feel responsible for others or a greater good, as the SJ does.

The SP is an adventurer who is impulsive and who loves change and exploration. They move on to another project completely and easily. It is the start-up that calls to them, not the follow-through. The SP gravitates toward work that involves action and tools, like being a logger, a mercenary soldier, a wilderness ranger, an ambulance driver, or a statesman. Freedom, independence, and action are keys to the SP's satisfaction.

For the SJ, it is about completing the project. The SJ is drawn to the follow-through and implementation of a well-designed system. The SJ is happily geared to repetitive organization using a proven system. SJs are often drawn to things with clear boundaries and rules of operation, like law enforcement, teaching, preaching, accounting, banking, and hospital management. These are all professions within institutions. They all have set patterns and clear expectations that the SJ can meet.

The SJ has a sense of being duty bound and obligated. More than any other type, the SJ hungers to be part of a community or to gain membership with others in a social unit, but he will not ask for recognition for his service or care. Seeking to belong is a strong driver for the SJ and the SJ's feeling of responsibility permeates his need to take on more and more. After all, if he doesn't do it, who will?

Within the general population, 38% is SJ and 38% SP

◑ SP and SJ Combinations

ISTP	ESTP	ISFP	ESFP
ISTJ	ESTJ	ISFJ	ESFJ

An S of any type is a solid student of the facts and of history. No matter the style of expression, they will look for and pay attention to the details and appreciate staying focused on what they feel is reality. How reality became what it is seems to be explainable for the S by looking at the past. Data that is tangible and can be collected based on fact has value to the S. No matter what their other letters and preferences are, this part will be true for them. It is as a sensing (S) person that they view the world, and they will remain sensible by nature with a no-nonsense approach.

CHAPTER NINE

Intuition (N): NT and NF Combinations

SIMILAR TO THE S PERSON'S NEED TO PARTNER WITH EITHER THE J OR THE P TO sort out the details, the N person demands a partner as well. The N is always teamed up with either the T or the F. While the SJ depends on knowing how to organize data into a system or a policy and the SP depends on expressing the data in an art piece, music, or in creative writing, the N is not interested in either of those realms. Instead, the N depends on making choices or decisions from the information they have intuited.

The NF wants to feel into the choice and be real and authentic while doing so, whereas the NT wants to make choices based on rational thought.

While SJs and SPs are commonly surrounded by other SJs and SPs in their working and living environment due to their sheer numbers (38% of each in the general population), the NTs are rarely with their own kind and may feel like an alien. Even their parents are more than likely to have the S as their preference.

The NT respects intelligence. Under the surface of every NT lies a scientist who is querying nonstop, often asking the questions others have not thought to ask. The most descriptive word for the NT is "competence." The NT believes that they *must* be competent. The NT is the most self-critical of all the categories. While the SJ is full of "should" and "ought," the NT takes it to the level of "should know" or "should be able to" in their head. They are often individualistic, indifferent, and even arrogant.

NTs are harder on themselves than any other pairing. They must be competent in what they pursue and will settle for nothing else. Self-doubt is the NT's nemesis. It can paralyze them when it is time to take action, particularly if combined with the P.

While their natural arrogance does not endear them to the hearts of others, it can produce documents and works that influence the thinking of social groups or countries. When the NT speaks, they avoid redundancies. Their style tends to be compact and logical with no effort made to point out what seems obvious. At times they can be obtuse to the meta-messages in the communications of others. Preciseness in language is their preference.

The NT is never willing to repeat an error, yet once they master a technology or challenge, they move on to something else. At times, the NT can be oblivious to the emotional responses of others, lacking sensitivity to the complexity of another person's feelings and offering critique without feeling into how it will be received. They will focus on whether the critique is understood by the other, not how it feels to be on the receiving end of it. Because of that, an NT's critique is often accurate but feels as if it has been driven like a stake through the heart.

By contrast to the NT, the NF wants to feel into the choice and be real and authentic while doing so. They do not feel much need to explore how to organize the information, but focus more on formulating what action or decision to take. Their desire is to make the decision that will lead them into forming their vision of the future.

> **The NT is represented in the general population at 12% and female INTs make up less than 1% of the general population. Kiersey estimated that in a school classroom of thirty-two students, four might be NT with only one of them being an INTJ or INTP.**

The NF is an intuitive feeling person. These are the people known to champion others and inspire the people around them to believe in their own possibilities and reach higher. A natural coach, the NF is in a constant search for "self." Although not easy to put into words, their drive for self-actualization is so strong that they often fail to see the purposes of those in the other major groupings: SP (freedom), SJ (productivity), and NT (competency).

The NF has a pursuit with a strange end, a self-reflective end that defies itself as an end: becoming. While the SP, SJ, and NT often move toward goals in a straight line, the NF's search for self is circular and, thus, perpetual. The NF can never truly be herself since the very act of reaching for the self is a search for a moving target: becoming. Being true to herself is, therefore, always in motion and not fixed. It could be said that the NF sees herself as a verb, not a noun. To exist, the NF needs a clear identity and needs to make a difference. For her unique contributions to be recognized and appreciated means more to the NF than simply receiving remuneration.

The NF seeks to have no façade, no mask, and no pretense. They seek to remain genuine in all interactions. Harmony is a requirement in their life and they will go a long way to create it. Seeking a life of significance and making a difference in the world is often their plan with work. Unlike the NT, who lacks sensitivity to others, the NF is hypersensitive to the subtleties in gestures and metaphoric behavior.

The NF will put boundless time and energy into relationships. They are natural coaches and inspirers of others. Even though they make up only 12% of the population, NFs have a greater impact than that percentage would suggest because many are fluid communicators who become writers, motivational speakers, psychologists, and counseling ministers. They can also

be found in the Peace Corps, at horse rescue organizations, and in other causes that benefit mankind.

While the NT has a scientific, technical mindset, the NF is inspirational and queries the meaning of life. The concept that the search for meaning is a necessary drive for all mankind is spurred on by the NF, who is a bit mystified why the other types are not more curious or taking more interest in these pursuits. They tend to see potential in everyone but they may invest time and energy in those who are not self-directed and never intend to grow or become the person the NF sees as possible. This can result in pain and disillusionment for the NF when that person isn't interested in their help and attention.

In projects, the NF has boundless energy and commitment. Yet, the NF can be an intellectual butterfly adeptly moving from one project to the next. Like the SP, the NF wants to taste all of life, but unlike the SP, it is not merely for the event itself, but for the growth or self-understanding that can be gained from the experience.

As with the NT, the NF is future oriented, but while the NT is interested in analysis and critique, the NF is interested in the possibilities for lessons and growth. The NF is charismatic and more interested in interaction with people and connection than things. They seek cooperation rather than competition, and they are natural coaches who enjoy bringing out the best in others. They easily inspire those around them to reach for a better life or higher ground.

. . . .

NFs make up 12% of the general population. The NF understands that the visible world is only a part of what is real.

. . . .

⊙ NT AND NF COMBINATIONS

INFJ	INTJ	INFP	INTP
ENFP	ENTP	ENFJ	ENTJ

Contrary to the S (sensing) types, who are focused on reality and what is, the N (intuitive) is focused on possibilities. The reality the S values is seen by the N as a springboard to the future. The N searches for meaning and a personalized vision of the road ahead. Ns have no real means to explain how they distill information from data. Often they do not try. They know their truth and trust it as solidly as the S trusts hardcore data or facts. While the S depends on perspiration, the N is more likely to depend on inspiration. The N lives with an ongoing sense of anticipation. They believe that everything can be improved upon, and they will always explore the route to doing so.

If you find yourself at odds with someone,
ask yourself if they are processing the
situation differently than you.

CHAPTER TEN

Putting It All Together

WE HAVE LOOKED AT THE INDIVIDUAL PREFERENCES FOR EACH PREFERENCE pair, shown on each column of the sorter answer sheet, and have looked at the key preference combinations. Now look at your own score again. What can you determine about yourself? Look at the strength or level of the numbers in each area, then envision the wonderful combination that defines you.

In Chapter One you met Sandy and Marnie. Now go back to Chapter One and reread about them. Can you establish what type each is?

Spoiler Alert: The answers are revealed below.

Sandy, an ISTJ, often observes the depth of a situation and can recall the specifics later while Marnie, an ENFP, takes in the entire environment. Let's continue following Marnie and Sandy.

Extroversion (E)/Introversion I): How we orient to the social world and our style of distilling thought.

Sensing (S)/Intuition (N): How we learn or absorb information and the type of information that attracts us.

Thinking (T)/Feeling (F): How we govern our choices and decisions, head or heart leading the way.

Judging (J)/Perceiving (P): How we organize our use of time and our environment.

"Have a nice day" means
"Have an interesting day" to an NT;
"Have a productive day" to an SJ;
"Have a fun day" to an SP;
"Have an inspiring day" to an NF.

Both Marnie and Sandy are chosen by their company to attend a large convention out of town. Both are excited. Sandy arrives at the airport with plenty of time to get her boarding pass and go through security. She has brought a novel on her iPad and is looking forward to a bit of relaxation time before the convention craziness takes off. She chooses a quiet restaurant near the gate and orders breakfast. She is quite content with her coffee, her food, and her novel. As she waits for the plane, she goes through her checklist one more time. She has an extra thumb drive, plenty of space on her iPhone for pictures, and clothes for any weather shift. Sandy looks for Marnie in the terminal but does not see her.

After paying her tab, Sandy goes to her gate, boarding pass in hand. She organizes the items she wants with her on the flight so she can stow her carry-on bag when she boards. Thirty minutes before the flight is scheduled to take off, she boards and gets settled in her seat. A steady stream of people board, but Marnie does not seem to be among them.

Finally, Marnie appears. She is so late that only one more person boards after her. When Marnie gets settled, she laughs as she tells Sandy that her alarm did not go off at the correct time, and she had forgotten she needed to drop off her cat at her neighbor's house for care while she is away. "Oh well," she says as she finishes her story, "I made it."

They both enjoy the conference, and on the flight back home, Marnie says, "Boy, I wish I could remember the way the keynote said that part about . . ."

Sandy not only knows the keynote speaker's name and title, she can also quote the line in question, verbatim—and does, to Marnie's surprise. Marnie had been worried about Sandy during the conference because it did not appear that she was having a very good time, and Marnie likes it best when they are both in harmony.

Marnie's energy rose as she attended all the parties, cruised the entire expo, met all the book reps, and made tons of new networking contacts. Fortunately, she had

remembered her stack of business cards and jammed them into her suitcase at the last minute.

A part of Sandy regrets not hanging in and seeing all the sights. Instead of making contacts, Sandy was in her hotel room each evening with a wonderful room service meal. She also focused on the notes she took at every session, capturing core content, and read an excellent book by the keynote.

Marnie took in how the event was pulled together and picked up loads of ideas for the company to use in creating new displays for regional expos. Sandy picked up on the depth of the material presented and created data spreadsheets and conference notes to e-mail her boss.

Are you beginning to see how this all fits together? Next, we'll look at the sixteen types, along with the characteristics frequently associated with each.

. . . .
Remember, there are sixteen possible combinations.

ISTJ	ISFJ	INFJ	INTJ
ISTP	ISFP	INFP	INTP
ESTP	ESFP	ENFP	ENTP
ESTJ	ESFJ	ENFJ	ENTJ

. . . .

The Introverts

As your understanding of each preference (represented by the letters E, I, N, S, T, F, J, and P) crystalizes and you grasp the key combinations, you become ready to explore the sixteen types in more detail. For instance, what is the difference between an introverted and an extraverted STJ? How does an extraverted NTP differ from an introverted NTP?

In this chapter, we will examine key elements of the eight I types, in all of their forms.

Introverts are likely to hold back when faced with something or someone unfamiliar. They seek time to process. That often requires allowing them some space and the freedom to enter into the conversation or situation when they feel comfortable. With their families and with those they have the chance to become comfortable, they can be more expressive. The introvert is interested in a limited number of relationships in which they can seek out depth in their interactions and focus on the internal reactions

The introvert (I) has a natural strength in writing more than speaking, especially when compared to an extravert (E).

of themselves and others. Let's look at how this dynamic affects the combinations of both the Sensing S personality and the Intuitive N.

◐ I S T J

The following are characteristics common to the ISTJ.

- Serious, quiet
- Earn success by concentration and thoroughness
- Practical, orderly, matter-of-fact
- Logical, realistic, and dependable
- Make up their own minds as to what should be accomplished
- See to it that everything is well organized
- Take responsibility
- Work towards their task steadily regardless of protests or distractions

The ISTJ type makes up about 6% of the general population. Their guiding principle is to be dependable. If an ISTJ agrees to take care of something for you, you do not need to check in with them about it. It is as good as done. Their word is their bond. These quiet and serious individuals have a keen interest in details, justice, and the practical procedures in life and work. They are patient with procedures and tasks but are not always patient with people. Duty to family, country, and institutions is never shirked although in family matters, they may see their duty as breadwinner or caretaker as necessarily superseding verbal or demonstrative support.

⊙ I S T P

The following are characteristics common to the ISTP.

- Cool onlookers; quiet and reserved
- Observe and analyze life with detached curiosity and unexpected flashes of humor
- Usually interested in impersonal principles
- Interested in cause and effect
- Interested in how and why mechanical things work
- Exert themselves no more than they think necessary
- Don't like to waste energy or be inefficient

The rare ISTP type makes up 1% of the general population. These duty-bound individuals are often fearless, risking themselves for the greater good more than any other type. That "greater good" may be on behalf of their country or city, a cause, or something as simple as an outing. They are drawn to tools of all kinds—from lasers to lathes and from supersonic jets to riding lawnmowers—and often master their use, becoming tool artisans. They communicate through action more than through words and will take a break to play on impulse. That play may be a run through open space, a spur of the moment fishing excursion, a trip on the open road, or anything else that allows them to feel free. Although something of a loner, at play the ISTP gravitates towards those who love the same kind of activities they do.

Where verbal communication is concerned, their conversation is sparse, direct, and can even be considered terse at times.

◉ I S F J

The following are characteristics common to the ISFJ.

- Quiet and friendly
- Responsible and conscientious
- Work devotedly to meet their obligations
- Lend stability to any project or group
- Thorough, painstaking, and accurate
- May need time to master technical subjects; interests are not usually technical
- Patient with detail and routine
- Loyal
- Considerate and concerned about how other people feel

The ISFJ type is found in 6% of the population. The guiding principle for these individuals is to be of service and to minister to the needs of others. Carrying a deep sense of history, the ISFJ values traditions highly. The environmental green movement with its focus on conservation is a natural cause for the ISFJ. Handbooks, rules, policies, and established procedures are closely followed and never questioned. While they will keep it to themselves, the ISFJ is annoyed by those who violate the rules, policies, and procedures. This may be the person in the supermarket express lane who is annoyed by the person with twenty items in their cart when the sign clearly says that the express lane is limited to those with no more than fifteen items.

ISFJ women have a flair for home décor, the culinary arts, and a clean and welcoming space. They are super-dependable and can be counted on, but they often find themselves taken for granted and may harbor feelings of resentment about that fact rather than clear the air.

ISFP

The following are characteristics common to the ISFP.

- Retiring, quietly friendly
- Sensitive, kind, and modest about their abilities
- Shun disagreements
- Do not force their opinions or values on others
- Usually do not want to lead but are often loyal followers
- Often relaxed about getting things done because they enjoy the present moment
- Do not want to spoil the "now" by undue haste or exertion

The ISFP is represented in 5% of the population. They are often found in the fine arts fields by career or avocation. The ISFP does not express themselves through direct verbal communication, preferring action. Because of this, they often confuse their partners in a relationship. They often feel invisible because their character and personality is not easy to discern by talking with them. Instead, who they are is expressed through their art. Kindness is one of their main traits and they are especially sensitive to the pain in others.

INFJ

The following are characteristics common to the INFJ.

- Quietly forceful
- Conscientious; succeeds by perseverance
- Concerned for others
- Puts their best efforts into their work

- Possess originality; desires to do whatever is needed or wanted
- Respected for their firm principles
- Likely to be honored and followed for their clear convictions
- Wants to serve the common good

The INFJ type makes up a mere 1% of the population. These are people who exhibit a strong drive to contribute to the greater good. They tend to have complicated, deep personalities, which sometimes makes getting to know them difficult. But because they are empathic by nature and therefore highly aware of the feelings of those around them, they exude personal warmth. The INFJ can also be a master of the metaphor, making them a powerful writer. Their insight, originality, and convictions help the INFJ excel at whatever they do.

INFP

The following are characteristics common to the INFP.

- Full of enthusiasm and loyalty but seldom talk of these until they know you well
- Care about learning, ideas, and language
- Enjoy independent projects of their own
- Tend to undertake too much but somehow get it done
- Friendly but often too absorbed in what they are doing to be sociable
- Little concern with possessions or physical surroundings

The INFP type, comprising 1% of the general population, moves quietly through the world and is usually seen by others as pleasant, but also shy or reserved. They have a profound sense of honor and adhere to their ideals above all else. In fact, if their ideals are violated, they will not budge and relationships will be forsaken. But INFPs are otherwise adaptable and seek unity in all areas. They welcome new people and new ideas, and they are sensitive to the emotional world of those around them. Whatever they undertake, they are willing to apply themselves to it.

INTJ

The following are characteristics common to the INTJ.

- Usually have original minds and great drive for their own ideas and purposes in fields that appeal to them
- Have a fine power to organize a job and carry it through with or without help
- Skeptical and critical
- Independent
- Determined
- Often appear stubborn
- Must learn to yield less important points in order to win the most important

Though they only make up 1% of the general population, the INTJ type makes a strong impact. They are the most self-confident of all the types. They see reality as something to be changed and usually have in mind a great starting place for doing so. Those characteristics are joined by a strong drive to complete what they begin and the ability to rise to challenges in creative ways. INTJs can be single-minded and often make coworkers feel as if they see right through them. They can be guilty of ignoring those around them. It is not obvious to those interacting with the INTJ that their most important preference is intuition. Instead, what they clearly see is the INTJ's intellect and the fact that the INTJ often asks questions that others do not even think of asking.

◑ I N T P

The following are characteristics common to the INTP.

- Quiet and reserved, impersonal
- Parties and small talk hold little appeal for them
- Enjoy theoretical or scientific subjects
- Logical to the point of splitting hairs
- Usually interested in ideas
- Tend to have careers where some sharply defined interests can be useful

Comprising 1% of the general population, the INTP type is filled with intellectual precision. Inconsistencies jump out at the INTP before anyone else notices them. They are the visionary architects who show brilliance in the planning and the startup phases of projects. It is necessary for them to have a team who will attend to the details and follow-through because the INTP is quickly bored with those things and will never do them. They will be on to the next complex situation to conquer. INTPs are frequently misunderstood and can seem difficult to know. They can also be quite unaware of the needs of others. With no tolerance for redundancy, they can be poor team players lacking patience in the processing styles of coworkers who like to rehash things.

The introverts combine with the other preferences and interact and express themselves after taking the time to distill their thoughts. They have a strong need for space and solitude to recharge their batteries and will appreciate time to prepare their thoughts before speaking. All introverts need and seek personal space to be happy. In conversation, they appreciate depth.

Now that we have explored the introverts, let's take a look at the extraverts.

CHAPTER TWELVE

The Extraverts

THE SOCIALLY OUTGOING EXTRAVERT NEEDS TO EXPRESS THEIR THOUGHTS verbally. By doing so, they can distill them down to what they mean to convey.

⊙ E S T P

The following are characteristics common to the ESTP.

- Matter-of-fact
- Do not worry or hurry
- Enjoy whatever comes along
- Tend to like mechanical things and sports with friends
- May be a bit blunt or insensitive
- Adaptable and tolerant

. . . .

The extravert (E) has a natural strength in verbalizing over writing, especially when compared to an introvert (I).

. . . .

- Generally conservative in values
- Are best with real things that can be worked or handled (taken apart or put together)

These are the men and women of action. The ESTPs make up about 13% of the general population, and when they are present, everything gets going. They are resourceful, witty, clever, and fun. Life is never dull around an ESTP. The ESTP has an uncanny ability to observe others and know their motivations. They are initiators of enterprise who are capable of rallying the troops and pulling teams together. But they are not there for long. Once the team is functioning and the enterprise has been established, they are ready to move on to the next challenge. Their desire to live in the immediate moment leads to excitement, but they are challenging mates if you are looking for anyone steady because the ESTP often lives by the motto, "He who travels fastest travels alone."

ESTJ

The following are characteristics common to the ESTJ.

- Practical, realistic, matter-of-fact
- Have a natural head for business or mechanics
- Not interested in subjects they see no use for
- Can apply themselves when necessary
- Like to organize and run activities
- May make good administrators, especially if they remember to consider others' feelings or points of view

At 13% of the general population, it is the ESTJ who tunes in to their community and takes on responsibility easily. Outstanding at organizing and following set rules, policies, and procedures, the ESTJ tends to be impatient with those who do not live by the rules. They are realistic, matter-of-fact, and attracted to time-honored traditions. The ESTJs are dependable, consistent, and loyal to their families, institutions, and community. But they are usually only interested in their own point of view, so they must make an effort to listen to input from others. The ESTJs are easy to get to know and clear in their communication. They do not send double messages.

ESFP

The following are characteristics common to the ESFP.

- Outgoing and easygoing
- Accepting and friendly
- Enjoys much and makes things more fun for others by their enjoyment of them
- Likes sports and making things
- Knows what's going on and joins in eagerly
- Finds remembering facts easier than mastering theories
- Best in situations with people or things that need sound common sense and practical ability

This type, which radiates warmth and optimism, makes up 13% of the general population. They are great fun to be with because they are open, clever, witty, and generous. The ESFP will avoid being alone. They are performers who seek the company of others whenever possible. They display their joy in food, drink, entertainment, and all of the finer things, creating a good mood wherever they go. Viewing life as abundant, the ESFPs are often generous to a fault. Because they prefer active jobs with interaction and thrive in the limelight, they should never be on solitary assignments.

◉ E S F J

The following are common characteristics of the ESFJ.

- Warmhearted, talkative
- Popular, born cooperators
- Conscientious
- Active committee members
- Need harmony and may be good at creating it
- Always doing something nice for someone
- Work best with encouragement and praise
- Little interest in abstract thinking or technical subjects
- Main interest is in things that directly and visibly affect people's lives

The most sociable of all types, the ESFJ is energized by interactions. They make up 13% of the general population. Harmony is a key to this type. Great nurturers, they enjoy entertaining and are outstanding hosts and hostesses, assuring that all are comfortable and attended to. ESTJs want their family life to be scheduled, routinized, and efficient. They need to be needed and loved, wear their hearts on their sleeves, and are outgoing in their emotional reactions. They idealize whomever they admire. The ESFJ lives for people and things rather than ideas and principles.

◉ E N F P

The following are characteristics common to the ENFP.

- Warmly enthusiastic
- High-spirited

- Ingenious and imaginative
- Able to do almost anything that interests them
- Quick with a solution for any difficulty and ready to help anyone with a problem
- Often rely on their abilities to improvise instead of preparing in advance
- Can usually find compelling reasons for whatever they want

To the 5% of the population that is ENFPs, intense emotional experiences are vital, and their feelings encompass both breadth of range and great variety. The ENFP scans the environment continuously and little misses their keen observation, though their attention is never passive or casual. They lack interest in the mundane routines of life. The ENFP can be accurate about their perceptions and then leap to the wrong conclusions. Being hyperalert, they often suffer from muscle tension. With their charm and outstanding intuitive powers, the ENFP is unusually skilled at handling people.

● E N F J

The following are characteristics common to the ENFJ.

- Sociable
- Popular
- Sympathetic
- Responsive and responsible
- Generally feel real concern for what others think or want
- Try to handle things with due regard for other people's feelings
- Can present a proposal or lead a group discussion with ease and tact
- Responsive to praise and criticism

Outstanding natural leaders, charisma rules for this type, which comprises 5% of the population. They place a high value on cooperation and place people as the highest importance or priority. Communicating caring concern and a willingness to become involved, the ENFJ is always on hand to lend support. This can lead to their feeling overwhelmed and vulnerable. Usually deeply devoted to their children and to their mates, the ENFJ relates to others with empathy. Teamed up with their intuition, which tends to be open and well developed, the ENFJ makes good and quick decisions when they trust themselves. They are socially adept and charismatic.

⦿ E N T P

The following are characteristics common to the ENTP.

- Stimulating company
- Alert and outspoken
- Quick and ingenious
- Good at many things
- May argue either side of a question, just for fun
- Resourceful in solving new and challenging problems
- May neglect routine assignments
- Apt to turn to one new interest after another
- Skillful in finding logical reasons for what they want

Sensitive to possibilities and not afraid to express out loud, the ENTP makes up 5% of the general population. Good at analysis, they exhibit an enjoyment of the complex. The ENTP remains alert to what may be happening next, is apt to have an interest in everything, and is always creating a better way of doing things. ENTPs are fascinating conversationalists who are able to follow and contribute to the most complex of discussions. They laugh easily, are gregarious, and are usually in good humor. Outwitting the system and the rules is enjoyable to the nonconformist ENTP.

◉ E N T J

The following are characteristics common to the ENTJ.

- Frank and decisive
- Hearty
- Leaders in activities
- Usually good at anything that requires reasoning and intelligent talk, such as public speaking
- Usually well-informed, enjoys adding to their font of knowledge
- May sometimes be more positive and confident than their experience warrants

The natural force behind the ENTJ is their ability to lead and command. They have a strong personality and even stronger will. Found in nearly 5% of the general population, the ENTJ creates or finds structure wherever they are. Following procedures can be tolerated by the ENTJ, but they will abandon any that they see as failing to lead to their goal. Repetition of error makes them impatient. For the ENTJ, there must always be a reason for doing anything, and a personal feeling is never a reason. The ENTJ takes charge of their home when they are present, leaving no doubt who is in control. They expect a great deal from their mates and children.

We have now looked at all sixteen types. Each has distinct traits and preferences. These distinct traits and preferences impact how they communicate and want to be communicated with. When we understand this, we can hone our communication to provide more clarity and understanding. In the next chapter, we will look at suggestions for communicating with the major combinations.

Also, because there are such strong differences between the sixteen types, it makes sense that there would also be pet peeves or things that irritate a person according to his type. In the next chapter, we will also take a look at how the major combinations react under stress.

CHAPTER THIRTEEN

The Communication and Understanding Charts

WHEN WORKING, COMMUNICATING, OR EVEN RIDING WITH OTHERS, IT IS HELPFUL to understand your own communication style. In addition, if you are aware of the things that push your buttons, you can respond instead of reacting, thereby avoiding becoming annoyed or misunderstanding the person with whom you are communicating. Depending on your role, you may desire to shift your own style to better connect with a person whose type is different from yours. As your awareness grows about how all of this affects your peace of mind, your level of understanding, and what you focus on, you can decide what effort you want to put forth.

Later, when we apply this to our horses, a whole new world can open up for you.

The following charts are designed to quickly convey the unique traits, needs, and desires of each type sector. Let's break it all down, starting with communication.

⊙ CHART ONE

Some Communication Aids

Speaker   Listener

E → I   Let the I process before responding.
              Give the I time to be alone.
              Listen when they talk, they have something to say.

I → E   Let the E process out loud.
              Affirm that your needing to sometimes be alone is not a
                  negative reflection on them.
              Try to communicate a little more.

S → N   Listen to what the N is saying. It is part of the big picture.
              Don't overload them with detail. They need a framework.
              Don't assume that their head is always in the clouds.

N → S   Listen. What the S is saying is part of the here and now.
              Give the S some facts and details regarding an idea.
              Complete your sentences and alert them to changing the
                  subject.

The N needs the S to

Bring up pertinent facts
Notice what needs attention now
Face difficulties with realism
Apply experience to problems
Track essential details

The S needs the N to

Bring up new possibilities
Apply ingenuity to a problem
Read signs of coming change
Watch for new essentials
Have vision

Some Communication Aids

Speaker		Listener	
T	➜	F	Be careful about being too critical.
			Don't assume that Fs don't think.
			Validate their feelings; let them feel.
F	➜	T	Try not to be overly emotional. Ts will not listen as well.
			Don't assume that Ts do not feel.
			Don't try to make them vulnerable.
J	➜	P	Don't assume that a P has come to a decision. They probably haven't.
			Don't try to make them a workaholic. It won't work.
			Don't give them a book on getting organized.
P	➜	J	Don't assume that a J has not come to a decision. They probably have.
			Don't force a J to play. It will become work to them.

The T needs the F to

Remain detached

Be critical

Look at logical implications

Make hard evaluations

Find flaws in advance

The F needs the T to

Consider the personal implications

Forecast the feelings of others

Look at values and ethics

Consider extenuating circumstances

Compliment others

Temperament and Stress Issues

NF What they do under stress: dissociate

Causes: Insincerity or betrayal by others, feeling devalued or dehumanized, being treated impersonally

Symptoms: Mood swings, depression, dissociation, shutting down, muscle spasms, eating disorders, delusions

How to respond: Treat personally, validate their feelings and nurture the relationship

NT What they do under stress: obsess

Causes: Feeling incompetent, stupid, lacking in knowledge, or powerless

Symptoms: Obsessions/compulsions, blocking, stuttering, phobias, performance anxieties

How to respond: Give them a new project; affirm their intelligence and competence

SJ What they do under stress: complain

Causes: Being abandoned; experiencing insubordination from others, feeling needless, useless, and/or without a role

Symptoms: Depression, insomnia, worry, restlessness, intestinal problems; feeling flushed, faint, cranky, irritable, and/or sick; decreased passion

How to respond: Create a new membership or role for them to be productive in; make a policy for them to follow

SP What they do under stress: retaliate

Causes: Constraints; feeling closed in, trapped, clumsy, and/or graceless

Symptoms: Retaliation, revenge, passive-aggression, lying, becoming oppositional, defiance, addictions

How to respond: Provide opportunities for new action; increase change and novelty

⊙ APPRECIATION AND IRRITATION

What They Appreciate Most in Self and Others
S: The clever, casual way they look
Integrity
P: Creativity, grace, and flair in their activities
Bravery, endurance, adaptation, timing

Others' Actions or Expectations That Irritate Them
S: Being told how to work, micromanaged
P: Standard operating procedures
An uptight attitude; rigidity

How They Irritate Others
S: Being overly detail oriented; focusing on the trees and missing the forest.
Seeing the plan as definite, not flexible
P: Carelessness about details; focusing on the forest and missing the trees
Being unprepared at times
Springing the unexpected on others

What They Appreciate Most in Self and Others

S: Caution, carefulness, thoroughness, accuracy

J: How well their products meet standards

       Responsibility, loyalty, industry

Others' Actions or Expectations That Irritate Them

S: Those who do not employ standard operating procedures

J: People who do not follow rules and regulations

       Violated deadlines

How They Irritate Others

S: Communicating a doom and gloom picture

       Failing to speak in the positive

J: Harping on procedure and policy

       Being rigid and inflexible

       Complaining

What They Appreciate Most in Self and Others

N: Their ideas and vision; their innovation

T: Their knowledge and originality

Others' Actions or Expectations That Irritate Them

N: Doing something illogical

T: Violating reason and principle

       Inefficiency

       Overemotional responses

How They Irritate Others
N: One-upmanship

_T:_   Argumentativeness

Arrogance

Hairsplitting

A critical and/or sarcastic nature

What They Appreciate Most in Self and Others
N: That which is personal and sensitive

Uniqueness

F: Authenticity; connection

Realness

Relationship dynamics

Others' Actions or Expectations That Irritate Them
N: Being treated impersonally

F: Superficiality

Political game playing

Personal cruelty

How They Irritate Others
N: Being overemotional, or hypersensitive to critique

F: Always wanting to talk about feelings

Being sensitive to criticism

Being unwilling to "play the game"

Being easily indignant

Now you are armed with a general grasp of who you are in terms of type. Remember that this is a foundation for how you form your values and your decisions. The specific scoring of each area and its relative strength, your key combinations, and the effect of all four letters together provide a full introduction to who you are.

Just as you have a distinct type, so does your horse. If your work with horses is in the novice stage, this may come as a surprise to you. But seasoned horse people know that every horse in their care has a distinct personality with distinct preferences. The two horses across the aisle from one another are different from one another, and those differences may be great or small depending on their individual horse types.

Let's take a look at a horse you know very well to determine his type and explore the information this can yield for you when riding, training, and caring for him.

PART TWO

Our Horses!

I'm adapting, I'm adapting!

CHAPTER FOURTEEN

Our Horses

As Lauren is placing the halter over QT's neck, he stops and shakes from head to tail to get paddock dirt off of his sleek black-and-white coat before she takes him back to the barn.

While walking up the small hill as he is being led back to his stall, QT is very mindful of his hoof placement. He steps brightly alongside her. As they reach the barn aisle, QT neighs a hello to inform his barn pals that he has returned. He stops and waits for Lauren to open the latch to his stall door, observing her every move. His experience seems to be guiding his movements. He makes a quick assessment of which horses are already in their box stalls and looks to see if the feed cart is prepared to begin the feeding regimen.

Lauren walks into his stall and he follows her easily, then stands stone still with his head high to have his halter removed. Once she has left the stall, he darts out into his run where he can see the other horses enjoying the sun before dinner is served, nickers

to a few geldings, and plays "pretend stallion" games with his neighbors. During the day when he is out in the paddock, he is the first to greet every horse.

Lauren returns to the turnout paddock to bring in QT's best mate, Shadow. Much of Shadow's day was spent rolling in a little patch of mud. The mud is now stuck on his bay body, which he does not mind at all. He takes his time to walk over to Lauren, stopping a couple of times to eat a flower and investigate a butterfly. He loves being on turn out and has a special spot he usually hangs out in no matter where the herd is. Most of the time he actually prefers to spend much of the day by himself, near but apart from the herd.

Today he senses that Lauren is in a happy mood, but on other days when he feels her sadness or she is worried, he is the first horse to reach her. The grass no longer matters if he can bring comfort to her. On this day, he ambles up the hill next to Lauren to be led to his stall. Entering the barn quietly, he continues to move a bit while she is working to get the latch open. Shadow stands anything but squared under himself. His body is in a funny position and he just hangs out, waiting for her. Lauren goes into his stall, and he gradually gathers himself up to join her. He hangs his head so it's easy for her to take his halter off. After it is off, he rubs up against her as if wanting her to stay awhile.

The tractor starts up for dinnertime and QT is at his feeder waiting and paying attention to all the horses as they are fed. Meanwhile, Shadow goes out to his run to get in one more roll before settling in for dinner. After the pellets and grain are put in the bottom section and the hay is neatly put in the top grid of each stall, the horses begin to nosh.

QT finishes his pellets and grain, licking the feeder before starting on his hay. He pulls pieces of his hay into his mouth and eats, sometimes taking a break to go out to his run and check out what others are doing. He has a certain spot in his run for his poop.

Shadow eats his hay first, then the pellets. When he eats his hay, he pulls big chunks of it to the stall floor and drags some into his waterer. Poop is not relegated to any particular spot. Shadow's kindness is his most predominant trait. He is especially sensitive to the pain in others and gives freely with sympathetic impulsivity to the sufferer.

I have had the privilege of having hundreds of horses during my career, both of my own and in my care. Their different personalities and learning styles are a huge part of the fun and challenge in my life. They are a true gift. As a breeder, I have had the opportunity to use a system called Foal Alert and was present for the birthing of over 250 foals. Their personalities all showed up as soon as they appeared.

Some were nickering and neighing on their way out of their mom. Eager to meet the world, they explored the stall and everyone present when they were only a few minutes old. Others came in softly and remained quiet, mostly interested in connecting to their mama but also highly observant of the world around them and taking it all in.

As a breeder and trainer, Carolyn has also loved the unique personalities of each horse. We associate some traits with the horse's breed, but other traits are particular to the horse, quite apart from breed, just as humans exhibit cultural traits while having distinct personalities apart from those traits.

Along with raising, training, and showing Arabians, Andalusians, Paso Finos, Spotted Saddle, and Rocky Mountain horses, Carolyn has boarded as many as fifty horses at a time and given more than fifty lessons per week. She is personally drawn to horses with lots of energy and drive, those that express their questions and love human touch.

My personal passions have been Quarter Horses and American Paints. My first horses were Appaloosas and today I also have Gypsy Vanners. I'm drawn to horses with less fire, I suppose. I love a great athlete who is curious and heart-centered. With a ranch in Arizona that averaged sixty-five boarders of all disciplines and our ranch in Colorado where we housed our own horses plus about thirty-five boarders, I have had almost every breed in my care on my facilities.

Just as we delved below the social and cultural differences in humans to explore temperament and type, we will be doing this with horses. An extraverted (E) horse is vocal and loves to connect with their pasture mates, not doing well by himself for long periods of time. An introverted (I) horse needs some alone time and may relish having the end stall with only one neighbor or a paddock with enough room to go off by herself.

The sensing (S) horse is the observer, the realistic horse that loves routine and remains down to earth. They know their job and do it in detailed fashion. The intuitive (N) horse sometimes has their mind off somewhere else and can have quite the imagination. They may appear to be singing, "Lions and tigers, and bears—oh, my!" from *The Wizard of Oz* when on the trail, having an abundance of curiosity about what is ahead.

The thinking (T) horse can seem a bit aloof or impersonal. They are the thinkers and are often firm with others, wanting to both abide by the rules and have their own boundaries respected. If left too long to brood, especially a more extroverted T, these horses will chew the barn or exhibit some other stall vice. When learning a new task, they want time to think it through. The feeling (F) horse is sensitive to how both their handlers and their herd mates are feeling emotionally. Harmony in the barn or paddock is important to them. They love to be touched by humans and horses and find ways to express appreciation to their human partners, offering true devotion.

The judging (J) horse often has a routine, whether they are in the barn or at liberty. They have a methodical way of eating, eliminating, and showing up for their work. Departures on the halter or on their back are precise, as if they want to be efficient and avoid wasting time. They appreciate being fed at relatively the same time each day and tend to keep their stalls and blankets in good order.

The perceiving (P) horse takes life as it comes. Rarely in a hurry, they find time to stop and smell the roses and adore just hanging out. Precise departures when riding are not their thing. Although they can be trained to do so, they would rather feel the cue and ramp up the enthusiasm to respond. Their stall is often a mess with feed in the waterer. Bedding is for chewing or urinating on. So are blankets if they can pull them off.

◑ HORSE JOBS AND CAREERS

By and large, horses are willing partners, highly adaptable in their jobs or careers. Just as the MBTI and the KTS are used to help humans find out what careers would suit them best, we can suppose the same for the equine world. Similarly, just as ENTJs may be well suited to police work but find themselves doing less suitable work, horses may be well suited to certain kinds of work but find themselves doing work they are less suited for by temperament. In fact, that scenario is more likely for horses because they have less voice in the matter.

Let's look at a few examples. You are sure to think of more as you become familiar with this material.

As you might recall, the SP is all about freedom. They are impulsive and desire lots of action. The SP horse, then, would be the ideal cutting horse or ranch roping cutting horse. Each day of work, he is out to do his job, and the rider knows from experience that he can turn him loose to cut that cow as he reads it. The cutting horse will love all of the action entailed in that work and will use his instincts and impulses well to turn the cow back and chase him into a pen. The SP horse thrives on the freedom given to him by his rider.

The foxhunter or polo horse may also be an SP seeking action and freedom with a lot of variety in both training days and field days. Given a cross-country course designed with obstacles that challenge the horse to navigate his way through a changing pathway, the SP is never bored.

The competition reiner or the high-level dressage horse learns a series of complex movements that are beautiful in their execution and precision. The SJ would be a great fit for this. The movements are practiced in precise repetition at the home arena and then combined into complex patterns during competition. The rules and cues are clear and given to the horse in exactly the same way each time, so his data is collected in a clear manner. He knows his job and loves performing it responsibly for his rider.

Thinking of the differences between the SP and the SJ, we can see that the rodeo bucking horse that loves his job might best be an SP. Their deep need to achieve freedom of expression would be satisfied with the random draw that yields different opponents and the requirement of working in different arenas each time they go out to buck. The rodeo barrel racing champion would more likely be an SJ. Running a repetitive pattern that has no room for variation suits the SJ horse, who likes to perform his job dependably every time.

As a harnessed workhorse, the SJ would love his job in service and would appreciate being depended on to pull the wagon or plow. The expectations are clear and often repetitive. For instance, the SJ horse would enjoy pulling a hay wagon of feed through a dairy farm every twelve hours, day after day. The repetitiveness allows him to understand what is expected of him in service and helps him become proficient at the procedure. Similarly, the carriage horse who carries tourists through a park on the same path hour after hour could easily be the SJ, performing his service steadily and responsibly.

But the NF would bring lots to the carriage horse job as well. In that role, the NF would draw people to his head for a pet and be sensitive to the joy, laughter, or tears of his patrons, using his intuitive and natural curiosity to make the ride even more fun.

SJ horses are seen in the hippotherapy barns as well. These are steady horses who take their jobs seriously and can be trusted to stand stone still while the paraplegic is lowered in a harness saddle to their back. The SJ will wait for the word and signal to walk because he honors the importance of the rules and procedures.

A strong desire to do a job the same way each time, follow rules set forth, and work in safety—this is the SJ horse.

A few NFs find their way into hippotherapy and their talents are usually seen in the loving connection from the ground. Small children can safely give them a hug, and they may wipe a child's tears or give the child a shoulder to cry on while moving their lips or muzzle through the child's hair to bring a smile. The NF horse will feel innately drawn to a person who is sad on a certain day or has just come from a chemotherapy treatment. They may just stand quietly nearby or listen and keep a secret that is shared with them. This is the forte of the NF horse.

While the SJ would also be a super pleasure horse, in the ring or out, the NT would be the ones who excel in pleasure competition. They have fire and power, and they strive to gain competence in their job. Whatever job they take on, they desire to master it exactly.

This would also play out for a jumper who knows his job and lets out a buck in self-criticism if he hits a rail. He truly wants to clear the rails and has not found mastery or competence if he fails to do so. So while other types may become good jumpers, the NT will seek excellence of his own accord.

A good racehorse might be an S type. The horse's jockey trains and exercises him each morning on the track in a counterclockwise direction. But on race day, the horse runs in a clockwise direction as part of his cue to give it his all. The specifics and repetition of the routine speak to the S, not the N. The racehorse who would be truly happy with his job is the SP. Natural to his type would be his clever boldness, endurance, adaptation, and freedom seeking nature, which would make him the champion who loves racing.

The police horse could be an SJ who desires to be in service, but it is the NT who loves doing it. The NT has the innate ability to take in situations on all levels, not just at a literal level. Because of that, the NT police horse would read situational parameters in ways that might be missed by other types. The variety of work as a police horse would also provide opportunities for them to use their intellect to discern the best objective strategy in a given situation. In this job, the NT would seek mastery and competence, not just perform a duty.

The horses that excel in the work I train EGCM practitioners to do with their clients are helping the clients work through many kinds of present and past trauma. That work comes easiest to the NF, who is born to care. Although all types offer something unique and wonderful, it is the NF who intuitively feels the client's struggle or emotional pain and works to bring comfort and insight. Frequently, my horses pantomime their intuitive read on the clients, thereby assisting me in my work. The NF's ability to be very personal, showing up in authenticity and moving toward the pain, gives intimate assistance in the healing process.

Consider all of the roles our horses are asked to perform. What a wonderful gift from *equus* that most do so with willingness and become well suited to their jobs. But typology gives us clues about what the horse would excel at doing and what would fit his natural preferences. When a horse's innate aptitude is taken into consideration, he will have an easier time understanding what is being asked of him. That provides the most natural situation for him, which can mean less training time and a happier horse.

Ready to test your horse?

CHAPTER FIFTEEN

Taking the Equusology Sorter™

BEFORE YOU TAKE THE EQUUSOLOGY SORTER, HERE ARE SOME KEY POINTS AND a little guidance.

1. Find a quiet place where you will not be disturbed by a child, your boss, a cell phone call, or other interruptions. It takes the average person about twenty minutes to complete the questionnaire.

2. Take a quick look at the answer sheet. You will be making a check mark in box "a" or "b" for each question. Notice that the answers run from left to right, not down the page in columnar form, so the answer to question 2 will be on the same row as the answer to question 1, not below it.

3. Do *not* ask anyone else what the question means.

4. Answer *all* the questions as you go through the test without skipping any of them.

5. It is important to answer each question honestly, from the standpoint of who you think your horse truly is, not as you think or feel it "should" be answered. There are no right or wrong answers, just answers that reflect who your horse is.

6. Give the answer that fits who your horse is *most* of the time, not under specific situations.

NOTE: Multiple score sheets are provided for your use.

⬢ Equusology Sorter™ Questions

1. When your horse is in the round pen at liberty and another horse is brought to the side of the round pen, your horse will
   a. approach the horse and handler within seconds, including a horse he doesn't know
   b. approach only a few horses, normally known to him

2. When your horse is exposed to new objects, he generally
   a. shows great interest and wants to touch and investigate the objects
   b. is wary, questioning, and slow to show interest in the objects

3. Your horse prefers to
   a. be shown and directed on how to do things
   b. figure out things on his own with little direction

4. When your horse is exposed to a new skill during training and doesn't seem to understand what is being asked, he is most likely to
   a. react and remain controllable if treated with fairness
   b. remain quiet as if deciding what to do next and exhibit a kind spirit

5. While observing your horse in the pasture, he could often be described as
   a. unaffected by others' interactions or emotions
   b. friendly and congenial with most and in harmony with them

6. Your horse appears in the best mood if you plan your work with him
   a. on a schedule about the same time each day
   b. on a "whenever" basis, with no particular schedule

7. When your horse is running in the field with a couple of horses that are his buddies, he is more apt to
   a. run near a fence line or in a similar, observable pattern
   b. run impulsively in various directions with no observable pattern

8. At a horse show or all-day organized event, your horse is
   a. very attentive, has lots of energy, and is still alert at the end of the day
   b. becomes more and more fatigued as the day progresses; becomes inattentive and sluggish

9. When you are riding your horse in new territory, he is
   a. alert and willing to try new things
   b. more anxious when placed in a new environment

10. Your horse is often more motivated and responsive when you are
    a. repeating skills previously learned
    b. providing opportunities for your horse to expand his knowledge in different situations

11. When you have observed your horse being pushed around in the field, he seems to have a greater propensity towards being
    a. fair with other horses
    b. kind and gentle-spirited with other horses

12. When your horse is returned to his field with the other horses, he generally
    a. walks into the field expressing little attachment
    b. goes straight to the other horses for engagement

13. When you are late at feeding time, your horse
   a. shows great irritation
   b. takes the lateness in stride and begins eating with few signs of irritation

14. When you are removing your horse's tack and receive a phone call, does your horse become more agitated
   a. when you answer the call before the tack is all removed
   b. when you quickly remove all tack and then answer the call

15. When your horse is free grazing in his pasture with the other herd mates, he
   a. is usually in the middle of those he likes the most
   b. grazes long spans of time off to himself

16. When your horse is in training and taught in graduated steps, he
   a. shows great interest and exhibits little stress
   b. becomes distracted and bored very easily

17. When training your horse, does your horse seem to prefer learning
   a. direct communication with each task broken down into small steps
   b. by slow, gradual, introduction of the task while allowing sight and contact with each step

18. When your horse is in the company of other horses, he appears to be more
   a. aloof and shows little interest in them
   b. desirous of their companionship

19. When your horse is being a bit of a bully in the field, he
   a. bullies everybody
   b. only bullies a select few

20. When your horse is fed outside in the pasture with hay in multiple locations, he will
   a. pick a hay pile and remain there
   b. move around from hay pile to hay pile

21. When your horse is in the stall, he
    a. manages his hay consumption the same way each day
    b. has no routine, eats out of his hay rack, and sometimes pulls the hay out of the hay rack and eats off the stall floor

22. Your horse could be described as
    a. expressive, vocal, and/or busy
    b. quiet by nature; seldom mutters a sound or nickers

23. Your horse seems to absorb knowledge more rapidly when
    a. you use objects or natural terrain to encourage instinctive learning
    b. you perform a skill correctly and then repeat that skill in various environments

24. Your horse has a work ethic that
    a. is strong
    b. requires lots of encouragement and support

25. In the field with herd mates, you often see
    a. your horse standing apart from the others
    b. mutual grooming between your horse and another

26. During a hierarchical struggle with another horse, if your horse is the most dominant of the two, you will most likely observe
    a. a show of dominance until the other horse becomes submissive
    b. your horse make a point of dominance and then walk away

27. Your horse prefers
    a. to load in the same order and be tied in the same spot for each trip
    b. no particular order of loading or location in the trailer

28. When cleaning your horse's feet, he
    a. cooperates best and relaxes most when you clean his feet in the same order each time
    b. shows no resistance or preference regardless of the order in which you clean his feet

29. When your horse is released back into his field, he
    a. quickly joins others to touch or smell
    b. waits for others to approach him

30. When your horse is on a trail ride in a location he has not been before, he
    a. navigates over and through places that are very similar to those in other locations
    b. requires coaching and/or prefers a lead over new obstacles

31. If your horse is observing youngsters nearby or across a fence, he
    a. keeps a close and watchful eye on the young
    b. allows the youngsters to roam, frolic, and play, exhibiting no concern

32. When you are riding your horse, he usually expresses
    a. his opinions clearly
    b. a desire to please you

33. When you are interacting with your horse, you would describe him, overall, as
    a. set in his ways
    b. easygoing and gentle

34. When you are tacking your horse and someone comes over to talk to you, your horse
    a. expresses a sense of "let's get the show on the road"
    b. expresses an attitude of "let life happen"

35. If you are riding your horse in a riding ring and you stop asking anything of your horse, he is most likely to
    a. continue the pattern you were riding or stop and wait for further direction from you
    b. aimlessly wander around the arena

36. Often when riding amongst a group of other horses, your horse
    a. becomes more energetic and stimulated
    b. becomes anxious and wary, tires quickly, and exhibits unease

37. Your horse is more naturally drawn to
   a. touching or smelling objects
   b. observing things from a distance

38. Your horse
   a. likes to touch, feel, smell, and lick everything within his reach
   b. seldom touches anything on his own

39. When you are asking something new of your horse, he is more apt to
   a. resist in many ways if he doesn't agree with the task
   b. give in to your desires rather quickly rather than disagree with you

40. Your horse can be more easily convinced to do things by
   a. consistently providing clear directions within already established boundaries
   b. showing kindness, patience, and heartfelt emotions for him

41. When your horse is delaying being caught, he
   a. usually takes the same routes to stay out of reach
   b. chooses paths of evasion that can't be predicted by you

42. When your horse is in a field by himself, he
   a. has designated areas in the field where he drops manure but not under his overhang
   b. drops manure wherever he stands or grazes

43. In a field with other horses, your horse is more likely to
   a. have brief contact with many of them
   b. choose one or two he is comfortable with to have contact

44. Your horse prefers
   a. positive substantial stimulation
   b. a few positive experiences with less stimulation

45. Your horse seems most cooperative and content when he is
    a. repeating a well-mastered skill
    b. exposed to a variety of new activities, although few are perfected

46. When you are preparing for a ride, your horse prefers that
    a. you groom, tack, and get the job done
    b. you touch, stroke, and groom without haste, and tack slowly, methodically, and gently

47. When you correct your horse, he sometimes
    a. appears remote and undisturbed
    b. appears to take it personally and responds to you as corrected

48. When your horse approaches you, he
    a. walks toward you with purpose, not faltering
    b. often stops two or three times, as if considering something, before reaching you

49. When your horse is first stalled, he often
    a. settles right in and shows no anxiety
    b. appears uncertain and slightly anxious after the door is closed

50. When you lead your horse near a strange horse he is most likely to
    a. gravitate towards the horse with ears up
    b. show little interest in the other horse

51. Your horse is most engaged and attentive when
    a. repeating skills already learned
    b. being exposed to new ways to use skills already learned

52. Your horse often appears
    a. to exhibit behaviors from practice or past actions
    b. to be a quick learner of new things and show inventiveness

53. Your horse performs tasks he knows well
    a. pretty much the same for anyone with the same riding skills as you
    b. better for you than others

54. When you are placing support leg wraps on your horse, he is more inclined to
    a. move around, pick up the leg, and display curiosity
    b. cooperate if there is no discomfort and show little anxiety

55. When riding in a ring, if you lay your reins on his neck and remove all leg aids, he is more likely to
    a. continue in the direction you were going
    b. begin wandering around aimlessly in the ring

56. After your horse has been fed in his stall, he is more likely to
    a. stay at his feeding trough until all feed is finished
    b. eat awhile, then move around the stall, and then go back to his feed

57. If your horse observes another horse being led outside his fence line, he
    a. hurries to get to the fence line
    b. shows little interest in the horse on the other side or stands and observes the horse from where he stands

58. When you are observing or riding your horse, he often appears
    a. methodical with a good sense of reality
    b. passionate for new adventures

59. Your horse
    a. appears very grounded
    b. lives in anticipation

60. When a young, inexperienced yearling is introduced to a new herd, you are most likely to see your horse
    a. observe the interactions of others from a distance but not choose anyone's side
    b. intervene on behalf of the yearling by cutting other horses away from him

61. Once you have established clear boundaries with your horse, he
    a. seldom pushes outside the boundaries
    b. tests the boundaries on a regular basis

62. If you are at a show and your classes are spread apart, your horse is more likely to
    a. remain cooperative if you leave the saddle on in between events
    b. show appreciation for the saddle being removed and placed back on at a later time

63. You normally bring your horse into the stable in the morning. If you go to catch your horse in the late afternoon, your horse is more likely to
    a. come immediately to the gate to be caught
    b. come a few steps, stop and look at you, walk a few more steps closer, then stop to look at you again, and continue to do this before coming all the way to the gate

64. Your horse is more inclined to be in his stall
    a. with his head to the door
    b. with his head to the back corner and his rump to the door

65. Your horse appears to have more fun
    a. working hand-in-hand with you and is very attentive
    b. romping with other horses in the ring, attention changing from one thing to another

66. Your horse prefers to learn new skills
    a. one step at a time before progressing
    b. rapidly with lots of variety

67. Your horse exhibits
    a. detachment when being groomed
    b. appreciation and connection with you when being groomed and seems to like the attention

68. In the pasture, your horse is more apt to
    a. stand up for himself if he is being bullied
    b. be moved around a lot by other horses without exhibiting great resistance

69. When approaching a new obstacle on the trail, your horse is more likely to
    a. make a snap judgment about how to maneuver the obstacle
    b. delay a decision until he has looked at the obstacle from many directions and still exhibits hesitancy in following through

70. When your horse is tied for an extended length of time (and can see other horses), he is more likely to
    a. stand quietly because this is part of a regular routine
    b. show restlessness in being restrained and exhibit heightened awareness of other horses

EQUUSOLOGY SORTER™ SCORE SHEET

	a	b		a	b		a	b		a	b		a	b		a	b		a	b
1			2			3			4			5			6			7		
8			9			10			11			12			13			14		
15			16			17			18			19			20			21		
22			23			24			25			26			27			28		
29			30			31			32			33			34			35		
36			37			38			39			40			41			42		
43			44			45			46			47			48			49		
50			51			52			53			54			55			56		
57			58			59			60			61			62			63		
64			65			66			67			68			69			70		

1 [ ] [ ] 2   3 [ ] [ ] 4   5 [ ] [ ] 6   7 [ ] [ ] 8

E   I   **S   N**   **T   F**   **J   P**

EQUUSOLOGY SORTER™ SCORE SHEET

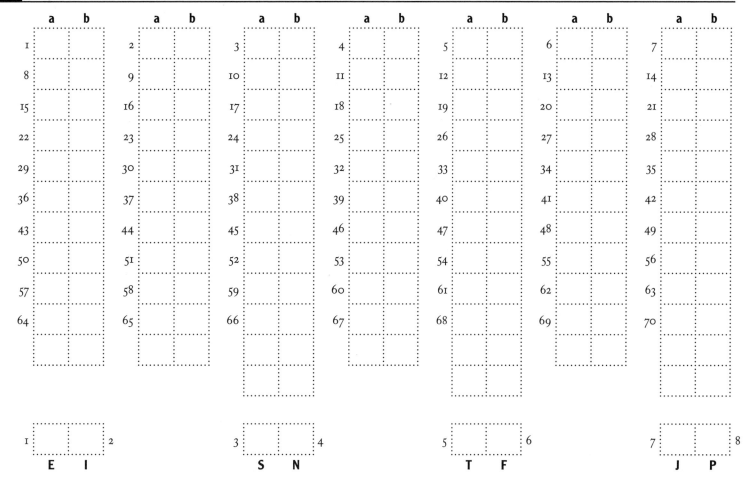

	a	b		a	b		a	b		a	b		a	b		a	b		a	b
1			2			3			4			5			6			7		
8			9			10			11			12			13			14		
15			16			17			18			19			20			21		
22			23			24			25			26			27			28		
29			30			31			32			33			34			35		
36			37			38			39			40			41			42		
43			44			45			46			47			48			49		
50			51			52			53			54			55			56		
57			58			59			60			61			62			63		
64			65			66			67			68			69			70		

1		2		3		4		5		6		7		8
	E	I			S	N			T	F			J	P

EQUUSOLOGY SORTER™ SCORE SHEET

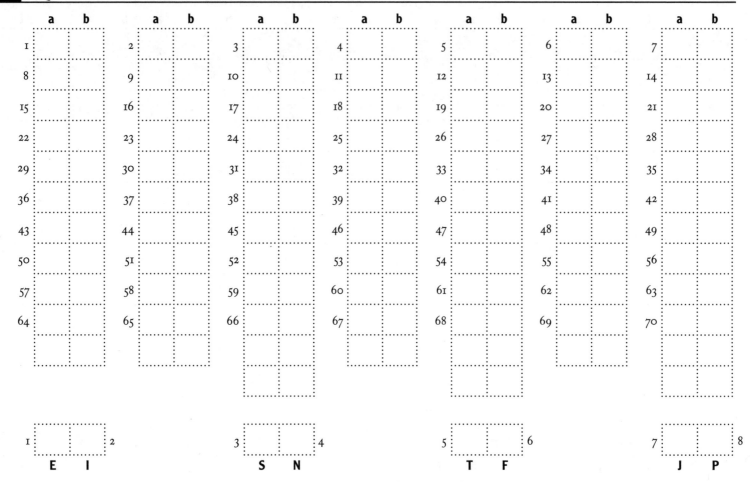

EQUUSOLOGY SORTER™ SCORE SHEET

	a	b		a	b		a	b		a	b		a	b		a	b		a	b
1			2			3			4			5			6			7		
8			9			10			11			12			13			14		
15			16			17			18			19			20			21		
22			23			24			25			26			27			28		
29			30			31			32			33			34			35		
36			37			38			39			40			41			42		
43			44			45			46			47			48			49		
50			51			52			53			54			55			56		
57			58			59			60			61			62			63		
64			65			66			67			68			69			70		

1			2		3			4		5			6		7			8
	E		I			S		N			T		F			J		P

Equusology Sorter™ Score Sheet

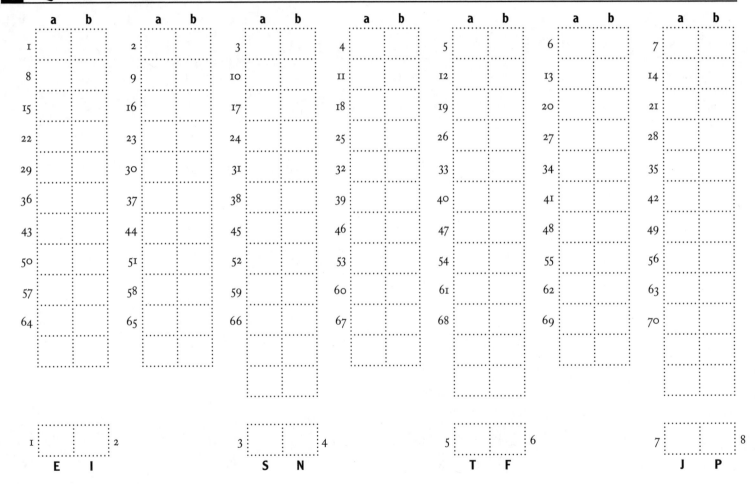

◯ DIRECTIONS FOR SCORING

You now have a check in either box "a" or "b" for each question.

1. Notice that the first row of blank boxes near the bottom of the answer sheet is numbered 1–8.

2. Add *down* each row so that the total number of "a" answers is written in the box at the bottom of each "a" column. Do the same for the "b" answers you have checked. Each of the 14 boxes near the bottom should have a number in it.

3. On your answer sheet, transfer the number in box #1 of the answer sheet to box #1 below (lowest box). Do this for box #2 as well. You now have a total number for the E and the I. The combined number for boxes 1 and 2 should equal 10.

4. As you continue bringing your answers down the columns across this row, notice there are two #3 columns, two #4, etc. Add each column *downward* placing the total number of checks in each column in the corresponding box number.

5. Each of the first set of numbers (i.e. first box #3 and first box #4) will be carried in the lower boxes under the second set of numbers so they can be combined into one total (just as you did for boxes #1 and #2). The two #3 numbers will be added together downward to provide the number placed in the lowest box and the two #4 numbers will be added together downward to provide the number placed in the lowest box. You should now have a total number for the S and the N. The combined numbers for the lowest boxes on the answer sheet should equal 20.

6. Now continue this scoring method, bringing down the total for each column first, transferring the first set of scores for those numbers to the lower boxes so they may be added for one combined total score. This process will provide you with one score

You have now identified your "type." It should be one of the following.

INFP	ISFP	INTP	ISTP
ENFP	ESFP	ENTP	ESTP
INFJ	ISFJ	INTJ	ISTJ
ENFJ	ESFJ	ENTJ	ESTJ

for the T, F, J and P. The combined numbers for #5 and #6 should equal 20 and the combined numbers for #7 and #8 should equal 20.

7. Now you have four pairs of numbers. Circle the letter below that is the larger number of the pair. If the two numbers of any pair are the same, then do not circle either number but put a large "X" below them and circle the "X."

If you have an "**X**" in your horse's type, his is a mixed type, which means his preferences are nearly the same between those types.

Having identified your horse's type, the task now is to read the type description and to decide how well or how poorly the description fits. If you have an "X" in your horse's type, his is a combination of two types, so you will probably find he has characteristics from each of the descriptions that are applicable for him. For example, if he is an "X" in the J/P category, you may find the "J" description fits him in some situations and the "P" description fits him in other situations. He may prefer closure on some things and like to leave options open in other areas of his life.

Now that you believe you know your horse's type, let's test it out with your horse, using some exercises.

CHAPTER SIXTEEN

Let's Have Some Fun: Test Your Horse

YOU HAVE TAKEN THE EQUINE VERSION OF THE TEMPERAMENT TEST AND NOW it is time to see if your horse would have answered the questions the same way. The exercises have been designed for you to observe your horse's preferences.

Exercises 1–6 will help you determine your horse's social preference: Extroversion (E) or Introversion (I).

Exercises 7–12 will help you determine your horse's preferred method of collecting data and their learning style: Sensing (S) or Intuition (N).

Exercises 13–18 will help you determine your horse's preferred method of making decisions: Thinking (T) or Feeling (F).

Exercises 19–23 will help you determine the way your horse organizes his time and environment: Judging (J) or Perceiving (P).

All exercises can be set up in minutes and need little other than your environment, a few objects, and a few extra horses to set the stage for learning more about your horse. Remember, it is very important not to influence your horse in any way when setting the stage for the exercises. Please complete five of the six exercises offered in each category.

The first category is valued at 2 points per exercise, so you will have a total of 10 points for social preference after completing five exercises. The remaining three categories have a value of 4 points per exercise, which means that when you complete five exercises, there will be a total of 20 points for *each* of the remaining preferences (collecting data/learning style; making decisions; organizing time/environment). By weighting each category in this manner, the scoring should provide calculations that are similar to the equine test you took for your horse earlier.

Remember to choose five of the exercises in each category. We have added an alternative exercise in each category in case you do not have an environment that makes an exercise easily staged.

There will be a question to answer once you have completed each exercise, and that question will have an "a" and a "b" answer. Place a check in the "a" column if your horse appears more "a" or a check in the "b" column if your horse appears more "b."

The score sheet you will use can be found at the end of the exercises.

🐎 EXERCISES 1–6

Determine Your Horse's Social Preference (E/I)

Exercise 1: Dining In
Score Value: 2 points
Needed:

- Round pen or other midsized enclosed space
- Horse you are testing and three to five other horses (a few your horse knows and others he does not know)
- A flake of hay

Approximate Time: 15–20 minutes

Place one flake of hay on the ground in the center of the round pen. Place your horse in the round pen at liberty and move away from the pen. Have someone lead a horse (not a stallion) near the outside edge of the round pen and watch your horse's reaction.

a. Your horse nickers when he sees the other horse approaching.

He approaches the corral fence whether or not he knows the horse.

You see his energy level increase when the horse approaches the fence.

b. Your horse only approaches the corral fence when he knows the horse being led nearby.

Your horse continues eating and shows little interest in the horse being led.

Your horse turns away from the horse being led.

Exercise 2: Who's Your Buddy
Score Value: 2 points
Needed:

- Large pasture or paddock with other horses in the area that your horse knows well

Approximate Time: 30–60 minutes
Make sure there is no grain or hay in the pasture at the time you set up this exercise. After stalling or confining your horse overnight, turn your horse into a pasture with other horses that know your horse. When you release your horse, watch his reaction.

    a. He goes straight over to the herd.
       He nickers or vocalizes his presence to the other horses.
       He appears comfortable in the middle of the herd.
       He stays put when others approach him.

    b. He waits for other horses to approach him.
       He enters the field and begins grazing away from the other horses.
       He grazes long periods of time to himself.
       When another horse walks over to him, he turns and walks away.

Exercise 3: My Room
Score Value: 2 points
Needed:

- Stall and other horses

Approximate Time: 15–20 minutes
Place your horse in his stall and walk away from the front stall wall. Now observe your horse. Return 20 minutes later.

a. He keeps his head facing the front of the stall.

   He stays at the front wall and looks outward with interest in what is going on outside his stall.

   When another horse your horse doesn't know walks near the stall, he turns to greet the horse.

   You leave the stall area, and when you approach the stall door 20 minutes later, your horse meets you at the door.

a. He gravitates to the back wall with his rump to the front of the stall wall.

   When another horse your horse doesn't know walks near the stall, your horse turns away from the unfamiliar horse.

   You leave the stall area, and when you approach the stall door 20 minutes later, your horse stays where he is or turns away from you.

Exercise 4: Day Trip
Score Value: 2 points
Needed:

• A small group of horses and horse riders to ride with

Approximate Time: 60 minutes

Tack your horse and go to the riding ring or hit a trail. Plan on spending at least an hour with at least four other horses and riders while you ride. Now pay attention to how your horse is reacting around other horses.

a. Your horse appears more energetic or stimulated with other horses nearby.

   Your horse asks to make brief contact with other horses, wanting to check them out.

b. Your horse becomes anxious or wary when another horse is nearby.

   Your horse appears more comfortable, or relaxed, with certain horses in his proximity than others.

Exercise 5: Merry-Go-Lunge
Score Value: 2 points
Needed:

- Lunge line
- Lunging area with other horses in sight

Approximate Time: 15–30 minutes

Put a halter on your horse and lead him to a lunging area in sight of other horses. Now put your horse through his gaits on the lunge line.

a. Your horse seems very aware of his external surroundings (he looks around while being lunged) and possibly nickers to other horses.

Your horse appears exuberant on the lunge line.

b. Your horse seems focused on you and not his surroundings.

Your horse seems focused on the task.

Exercise 6: The Runway Strip
Score Value: 2 points
Needed:

- Stall area
- Other horses, including some he doesn't know well

Approximate Time: 15–30 minutes

Place your horse in his stall. Walk other horses down the center of the aisle in front of your horse's stall.

a. Your horse shows interest in the presence of the other horses.

Your horse seems undisturbed by the activity of horses going down the aisle.

b. Your horse seems somewhat territorial of his stall (not wanting another horse nearby) when he sees a horse he doesn't know going down the center aisle.

Your horse seems less disturbed if the horse going down the aisle is a horse he knows well.

⏾ EXERCISES 7–12

Determine Your Horse's Preferred Method of Collecting Data or His Learning Style (S/N)

Exercise 7: Curious George
Score Value: 4 points
Needed:

- Enclosed arena
- Two large objects your horse has never seen, such as a large ball and a barrel

Approximate Time: 20 minutes

Place a couple of objects that your horse has never seen in an enclosed area. Spread them apart a little bit. Turn your horse into this enclosed area at liberty. Now observe from a distance.

a. Your horse appears wary of the new objects.

Your horse slows to show interest in the objects.

Your horse appears to show interest but from a distance.

b. Your horse shows almost immediate interest in an object and wants to investigate it.

Your horse stays near an object and wants to touch, smell, or lick the object.

Your horse quickly figures out how to manipulate the objects (such as moving a ball and turning over a barrel).

Exercise 8: Lions, Tigers, or Bears
Score Value: 4 points
Needed:

- A 3–5 mile trail that has not been ridden or walked by your horse before, but which is similar to other areas he has been exposed to before.

Approximate Time: 90 minutes

Tack/halter your horse and get ready for a trail ride or an outdoor walking experience.

    a. Your horse navigates the new terrain with ease.

       Your horse appears to be focused on the ground underfoot as if methodically covering each part of the trail.

    b. Your horse appears alert and motivated, very willing to go forward.

       Your horse appears passionate and energetic covering new terrain.

       Your horse appears to be happily anticipating what is ahead on the trail.

Exercise 9: Road Trip
Score Value: 4 points
Needed:

- Truck and horse trailer

Approximate Time: 30 minutes

Take your horse out near the driveway or into an area where you often load your horse into the horse trailer. Have someone drive the truck and trailer within sight of the horse and stop. Observe your horse.

    a. He appears to be saying, "Another day, another loading." He behaves as if he knows this routine.

       He gazes at the trailer without moving around or exhibiting anxiety.

    b. He appears to be saying, "Take me, take me. New adventures await."

       He appears more attentive and alert when the trailer first appears.

Exercise 10: School Day
Score Value: 4 points
Needed:

- 12' × 12' tarp

Approximate Time: 30–60 minutes

Your horse leads well and stands tied quietly. You are ready to teach your horse something new: to cross a tarp or stand on a tarp. Both feats can be performed mounted or leading your horse. Your horse has never been exposed to the new skill, assuming he hasn't walked on a tarp. If your horse has learned these, choose a skill that your horse has never had exposure to for this exercise such as an equine teeter-totter or bridge. Walk your horse in sight of the training site and now observe.

    a. Your horse appears wary of the object and requires additional coaching to go near the obstacle.

       Your horse needs clear directions from you when mastering an object.

       Your horse likes to be taught in direct communication, keeping each step small and gradually building up to navigating the object.

    a. Your horse appears enthusiastic and wants to go check out the area.

       Your horse wants to investigate the tarp or obstacle.

       Your horse seems more interested and motivated than normal when learning something new.

Exercise 11: Step It Up
Score Value: 4 points
Needed:

- Four poles
- Halter and lead rope

Approximate Time: 15–30 minutes

Lay four poles out in a straight row in parallel position with about 12 feet in between each pole. Bring your horse to the area. Begin leading your horse across the poles in a straight line near the middle of the pole. After you have crossed all poles, make an arcing circle back to the beginning and cross the poles again and again, keeping the same pattern. Keep your lead as long as you can while still keeping the horse centered in the poles. Observe your horse.

    a. Your horse seems more and more confident as you practice.

        Your horse steps with purpose after the first few crossings.

        Your horse appears focused on the task even though it is repetitive.

    b. Your horse wants to put his head down to sniff the pole(s).

        Your horse appears distracted by the stimuli in his surroundings, as if he is aware of much more than the exercise.

        Your horse's attention seems to drift or wander from the task after crossing the poles a few times.

Exercise 12: Ghostbusters
Score Value: 4 points
Needed:

- Area where your horse can be turned out by himself at liberty

- Opened umbrella
- 3' × 5' flag
- Swim noodles

Approximate Time: 15 minutes

Lay the objects around the outside of the enclosed liberty area, spacing them well apart. Bring your horse to the enclosed area and set him free. Watch his reactions.

a. He veers away from the edges, staying away from the outer fence lines where objects have been laid.

He stares at the objects for some time, appearing to evaluate them before moving closer to them.

If you halter your horse and lead him to one object, he appears to accept being close to one object more than having many to view.

b. He appears energized and enthusiastic by the new objects being nearby.

He quickly goes to the fence to check out one of the objects.

He moves on to other objects rather quickly.

◉ EXERCISES 13–18

To Determine Your Horse's Preferred Method of Making Decisions (T/F)

Exercise 13: Drag the Dragon
Score Value: 4 points
Needed:

- Cedar brush (any small bushy tree or bundled brush)
- 14 feet of rope

Approximate Time: 30 minutes

Attach the rope to the brush leaving approximately 12 feet or more of rope trailing from the brush. Walk your horse near the training area. When you get in sight of the area, closely observe your horse. Once your horse has investigated the brush, pick up the rope attached to the brush and lead your horse in a direction away from the brush, allowing the brush to trail behind your horse at a distance of 10 feet.

a. He remains quiet, as if thinking about what he should do next.

 Your horse reacts but remains controllable if you are treating him with fairness.

 When he is not agreeing with what you are asking him to do, he resists in multiple ways, but it appears that he wants to please you.

 He gives in to approaching the brush and having it pulled behind him pretty quickly rather than disagree with you.

 He depends on you for support and guidance.

b. He appears to want to please you.

 He gives in to what you are asking pretty quickly rather than disagree with you.

 He depends on you for support and guidance.

Exercise 14: Doing It My Way
Score Value: 4 points
Needed:

- Pasture with other horses

Approximate Time: 60 minutes

Walk your horse out to the pasture and release him. Now step away from the fence line and observe.

a. Your horse goes straight into the field with little attachment to any of the other horses.

He waits for the other horses to approach him.

Your horse seems aloof or unaffected by the interactions between the other horses.

b. Your horse goes straight to the other horses for engagement when he is released.

He appears kind and gentle-spirited with the other horses.

If your horse creates space between himself and other horses, it appears it is a select few.

Exercise 15: Clean As a Whistle
Score Value: 4 points
Needed:

- Quiet area
- Grooming tools
- One other person

Approximate Time: 30–60 minutes

Leave your horse loose in his stall and bring your grooming tools inside the stall with you or tie your horse in a quiet area where you normally would groom. Approach your horse and begin observing. One person will do the grooming while the other takes the role of observer. They trade roles later in the exercise. Do not rush this exercise between groomers.

a. Your horse appears to like the grooming done efficiently and in a timely fashion with small amounts of extra affection.

When you clean your horse's feet, he appears to respond more to getting the task completed than to showing the groomer lots of affection.

Your horse seems to respond similarly whether you are grooming or someone else is grooming.

b. Your horse likes gentle strokes of the brush with lots of human touch.

When another person is grooming your horse, your horse is less in tune with them than with you.

Your horse appears to appreciate the grooming time.

Exercise 16: Don't Rock the Boat
Score Value: 4 points
Needed:

- Tack
- Riding area with no other horses in close proximity
- Exclusive use of a riding ring

Approximate Time: 60 minutes including tack time

Tack your horse and ride out to the riding ring. Choose what you would like to work on during this exercise, such as walk-trot transitions, canter departures from the walk, standing still while mounting, etc., and observe your horse's reactions.

a. Your horse sometimes appears set in his ways and resists when he doesn't agree with what you are asking of him.

Your horse often works best within previously established boundaries, such as standing rock solid when mounting, because he has previously been trained to perform this way.

Your horse is more responsive when you communicate with clear, direct requests.

b. Your horse usually gives into your aid request rather easily.

Your horse seldom takes advantage of additional guidance and patience on your part.

Your horse would rather give in to your request than have you show your displeasure.

Exercise 17: The Lone Ranger
Score Value: 4 points
Needed:

- Tack
- One other rider of equal or near equal skill

Approximate Time: 30–60 minutes

Tack your horse and go into an area your horse is familiar with. Warm your horse up, unsaddle him, and then change riders.

    a. If another rider of near equal skill rides your horse, your horse's performance is close to the same as it was when you were riding him.

        If your horse appears confused over a cue or aid while being ridden by the other rider, he stops and plants his feet.

        If your horse is corrected by the other rider, he seems undisturbed.

    b. If another rider of near equal skill rides your horse, your horse's performance is not as good as when you are riding him.

        Your horse gives you a good try no matter what you are asking him to do.

        If you correct your horse, he becomes unsettled.

Exercise 18: Let's Make a Deal
Score Value: 4 points
Needed:

- Paddock or turn out area
- A couple of other horses

Approximate Time: 30 minutes

Observe the actions and reactions of your horse at liberty. Record which best describes your observations.

> **a.** Your horse makes a point of dominance until the other horse walks away.
>
>   If there is a young horse in the field, your horse stays clear of confrontation and doesn't intervene on behalf of the youngster.
>
> **b.** Your horse makes a point of dominance and then he walks away.
>
>   If there is a young horse in the field, your horse intervenes on behalf of the youngster and doesn't allow another horse to dominate him.

◉ EXERCISES 19–24

To Determine the Way Your Horse Organizes Information and Enjoys His Life (J/P)

Exercise 19: Come a Little Closer, Baby
Score Value: 4 points
Needed:

• Pasture

Approximate Time: 10 minutes, multiple times a week both at normal, routine times and at different times of day

Go to the gate and catch your horse on his established schedule for three days in a row and observe. Then switch the time you go to catch your horse at a totally different time and observe. Then go to the gate to catch your horse at random times and observe.

> **a.** Your horse comes to the gate more quickly if you have established a schedule and stick to that schedule.
>
>   Your horse walks directly up to you with clear purpose.

b. Your horse comes straight to the gate to meet you regardless of the time you go.

Your horse walks to the gate to meet you but often stops and looks around a little before arriving at the gate.

Exercise 20: Food for Thought
Score Value: 4 points
Needed:

- Stable

Approximate Time: 20 minutes

Place hay in the stall and then place your horse in the stall at a time he doesn't normally come into the barn. Step back away from the stall but remain in sight and watch closely.

a. Your horse appears anxious and less settled when you bring him in at a different time of day than normal.

Your horse has a routine way of consuming his hay and sticks to that routine.

b. Your horse settles right in and shows no anxiety when he is brought into the stable at a different time.

Your horse has no routine way of eating his hay.

Exercise 21: Going with Flow
Score Value: 4 points
Needed:

- Tack
- Grooming tools

Approximate Time: 60 minutes per time, repeated multiple times

For this exercise you will sometimes tack completely without interruptions. Other times you will tack with disturbances that create a delay in the tacking process or you may put the tack on and remove it in twenty minutes, repeating the tacking one hour later to observe if the horse exhibits any agitation around multiple tacking processes within a couple of hours.

   a. Your horse appears less agitated if you tack only once during the day.

     Your horse's mood is less positive when his routine is changed (for instance, when tacking was interrupted or when tacking was done multiple times during the day).

   b. Your horse seems unaffected if you leave and the task is not completed.

     Your horse expresses no agitation at being tacked multiple times throughout the day.

Exercise 22: Happy to Oblige
Score Value: 4 points
Needed:

- Truck and horse trailer
- A couple of additional familiar horses

Approximate Time: 30 minutes

Park your horse trailer rig in a location that is different from where you normally load the horses. Prepare to load the horses and observe. After mentally recording your horse's reaction to the trailer being in a different location, you will begin loading different horses on the trailer. Repeat the loading process but vary the order in which the horses are loaded.

   a. When the trailer is parked in a different location for loading than the normal spot, your horse seems to be more cautious approaching the trailer.

     Your horse prefers to be loaded in the same order each time.

     Your horse likes to be placed in the same location in the trailer or beside the same horse in the trailer each time.

    b. When the trailer is parked in a different location for loading than the normal spot,
          your horse seems to show interest in the new location but no negative reactions.
      Your horse seems to have little to no preference in loading order.
      Your horse seems to have no preference between trailer compartments.

Exercise 23: Rethink Routine
Score Value: 4 points
Needed:

- Paddock or pasture (by himself)

Approximate Time: 15 minutes, multiple times throughout the week
Keep your horse confined overnight. Place hay in the field in three different locations.
Walk your horse out to the paddock area and observe. Watch the departure pattern
your horse takes when he leaves the gate. Is it similar each time you release him or does
it vary from one release to the next? Watch how your horse chooses to eat his hay.

    a. Your horse runs in a similar pattern each time he runs in the paddock.
      When you feed your horse hay in the field in three different locations, your horse
          primarily stays at one pile until it is nearly finished and then moves to another pile.
      When you go to catch your horse and he is in the mood to evade you, he runs in a
          predictable pattern.

    b. Your horse runs impulsively in various directions in the paddock.
      When you feed your horse hay in the field in three different locations, your horse
          moves from pile to pile, eating from all the piles.
      When you go to catch your horse and he is in the mood to evade you, he runs in no
          predictable pattern.

Exercise 24: Whatcha Doin'
Score Value: 4 points
Needed:

- Stalls or another confined area

Approximate Time: 6 hours

Place your horse in a different stall than his own an hour later than normal. Observe his reactions to being placed in a different stall. Observe his reactions when fed later than his normal schedule.

  a. When you place your horse in a stall that is different than his normal stall, your horse appears slightly uncertain when you close the door.

When you place your horse's feed in his stall and he is being fed later than normal, he appears irritated with the delay in being fed.

Your horse drops his manure in his stall in the same location(s) each time.

  b. You notice absolutely no difference in your horse's attitude when you place him in a different stall than he is normally placed in.

When you feed your horse, he appears anxious for his food but not disturbed that it is later than normal.

Your horse drops his manure in his stall wherever he happens to be standing.

⬤ SCORE VALUES

In questions 1–6, each check represents a value of 2 points and in questions 7–24, each check represents a value of 4 points. Total each column to determine your horse's score. Note: You will record only five exercises in each category.

● SCORE SHEET

1–6		7–12		13–18		19–24	
a	b	a	b	a	b	a	b
a	b	a	b	a	b	a	b
a	b	a	b	a	b	a	b
a	b	a	b	a	b	a	b
a	b	a	b	a	b	a	b
a	b	a	b	a	b	b	b

We horsemen and horsewomen adore examining the personalities of our horses. How they are different from each other in terms of training and daily care is part of our discussions on a daily basis. Just like us, the sport of observing and conversing about them would not be interesting if they were all exactly alike.

CHAPTER SEVENTEEN

Case Studies

W<small>HAT FOLLOWS IS A COLLECTION OF REAL LIFE CASE STUDIES FROM</small> ECGM practitioners, graduates of the Touched by a Horse Certification Program. All who contributed stories were trained on the Keirsey Temperament Sorter and have experience partnering with horses for coaching work. These case studies illustrate how you can apply your horse's scores to real life with your own horse.

But it is not necessary to be trained on the Keirsey Temperament Sorter or necessary for you to partner with your horse for coaching to accurately determine your horse's score. Each case study contributor chose a horse they know well and summarized what that horse's personality type is based on their experiences with the horse. If they were unsure of how to score their horse's personality, they were asked to complete the Equusology Sorter test and then stage a few horse exercises. Lastly, they were asked to observe and document their horse's responses to further determine their horse's scores.

⬤ LONESTAR

A Seventeen-Year-Old Tennessee Walker Gelding

We have been partners for thirteen years.

When we met, we connected. As I loaded him into the trailer to bring him home, he was taking in every detail. I always snap the trailer ties to the cheek piece on the halter for safety. He took advantage of this straight away by leaning into the tie and using it to slip the halter off over his ears. He didn't try to escape, he just stood there observing to see if I had noticed his superior problem-solving skills. I am very attracted to this type of humor and knew that we were going to be great partners.

Lonestar has a witty, dry sense of humor and appears to be very standoffish as he evaluates you with laser-like focus from bottom to top. His skills as an escape artist are finely tuned and his tendency is to be easily bored. In my EGC work, people have reported that for some reason, they feel judged by him at the initial observation stage and don't usually choose to partner with him. He is a super-efficient lie detector, sensing whether a client believes what they are saying or not and doesn't enjoy drama from people or horses.

Mostly we partner for experiential learning with a client. The horse is at liberty and has the opportunity to join up with the client or not. He tolerates grooming because he is a sucker for the "beauty shop" rituals. He is efficient and direct when he chooses to partner in the EGC arena. He is not the first horse to volunteer for the work, and sometimes he doesn't even come in from the field. Sometimes he just watches the drama unfold and then swoops in to put the pieces in order at the end. He is very confident, and people say he looks like a "wiseass," which is probably mostly true.

My assessment is about an 8-I preference.

In the field, he is aware of where the other horses are but may or may not choose to graze in the same area. He doesn't mind trail riding with big groups but he certainly doesn't want anyone in his personal space. He has a very clear circular boundary space within which he keeps himself dead center.

Ear position is a clear indication of his tolerance for groups of people, but he is not a fan of group work. He enjoys grooming exercises and the safety demo (because this is his chance to evaluate the crowd), and he is a great model introvert for "contact" work with horses. He will invite you into his space when he is darn good and ready. He isn't rude if someone crowds his space, he just walks away with dismissive body language. Very rarely, he will throw in a tail swish depending on how much the person over-stepped his comfort zone.

He is about a 15-N preference.

His tolerance for step-by-step instruction is very limited. He gets bored really quickly and then moves right into troublemaker mode. I think he would become suicidal if I told him that he was going to be a lesson horse.

He expresses his ability to innovate in a variety of escape skills. He can untie any safety knot. Mostly, he chooses to stand still after the rope is untied. He just wants you to know he can do it.

He always takes a heads-up position in surveying what is around him. He doesn't get distracted by little things and can process a huge container of energy all at once with distinct clarity. I trust him to know exactly the safe route to take on the trail. He knows where his feet are at all times and navigates better than a compass. I trust him over my own assessment on trails every time.

Another 15 on the scale for the "T" preference.

Lonestar does not choose to snuggle into people who are blubbering or otherwise visibly emotional. He observes the process but doesn't like to hold that kind of space. He is very connected with the "T" process of emotions and stands firmly grounded, holding space for the humans. People often see this as cold and standoffish.

He is my personal rock because I am an 18-T and we understand each other's expression of emotions as they are processed in the brain. He is also highly efficient at distinguishing when a "T" person is thinking and when they are processing emotion through the brain channels. One time he observed an emotional outpouring by an F client who was very exhausted after her piece of work. He kept asking (insisting) to step up for this person, so I put him in the round pen and it was like that poster that says someday, someone will hug you so hard all your pieces will stick back together. He was a powerful emotional presence offering a clear container for this person to hold her pieces, even if she couldn't put them back together. This person gave me feedback two weeks later. She was still raving about how Lonestar made her feel and said it was like magic.

He is at least an 18-J.

His stall is perfectly tidy. He likes his feed pan in one place and he doesn't kick it around. He wants his hay in one place, and if you put it on the wrong side of the feed pan, he will paw it with his feet to the other side. When you are brushing his mane, he becomes a puddle of love unless you put part of the mane on the opposite side of his neck. If you do that, he will immediately put his head down and shake things back into place. He is also highly annoyed if his forelock is under the browband of the bridle. And while it seems hard to imagine, he watches with contempt when his stable mate dunks hay in his water bucket. Lonestar will not drink from a bucket that is messy. He has to be the first to drink if there is any bucket sharing.

Lonestar is an INTJ.
MICHELLE GRIFFITH (ES/NTJ), LEBANON, OHIO
www.ManeRiseCoaching.com

◉ SIR LANCELOT (AKA LANCE)

An Eleven-Year-Old Clydesdale-Quarter Horse Cross Gelding

Lance and I have been partners for two years.

I was first introduced to Lance through a photo. I immediately knew, without a shadow of a doubt, that we had been looking for one another for a long time. When Lance and I first met in person, he was a bit on the aloof side. He had traveled halfway across the country and was tired. He was quiet, calm, and really only interested in eating and resting. I assumed I had a quiet horse on my hands. I was wrong. Once Lance perked up and became acclimated, I started to see what he was really all about.

Lance loves to be around people almost more than horses. In the absence of people, he likes his herd. He is a very tall horse at 16.2 hands and upon first glance, he appears to be majestic, distinguished, and fluid. In reality, he is a kid in an adult's body with a wild sense of humor and a knack for opening the toughest of locks. He is also on the clumsy side.

Lance is a perfect match for the youth we work with on a regular basis. During EGC sessions with adults, Lance is quite different from the way he is with the youthful clients. He has little time for drama and little patience with clients who just aren't getting it as fast as he thinks they should. I love this about him because I see myself as a no BS coach. Together we are quite a team. He is the perfect partner for clients wanting to take action and move through their stuff quickly.

On the flip side, Lance needs a lot of support and direction. He isn't the most confident of horses until he has grasped his surroundings and what is expected of him. And he likes structure. Combine this with his no BS approach to healing work and he has a lot to offer anyone willing to step in the round pen with him—and, of course, a lot to offer me, his partner and person.

My assessment is about a 7-E preference.

If there is a person in the area, Lance looks for attention from them. Lance loves working with kids, and it seems the more, the merrier. But Lance loves other horses almost as much as he loves people. When he goes out to the pasture, he goes towards the herd. He will stay with the herd but he won't necessarily push his way in.

During EGC work with the round pen, he is a bit on the irritated side until someone finally steps in with him. On the rare occasion he needs to be stalled, he must have other horses or people in his line of sight or the stall doors take a pounding. The minute anybody walks by, he is at the door waiting and hoping they are there for him—horse or human. When at liberty in the arena, Lance has been known to snake his neck and swish his tail if there isn't any stimulation. He likes action and interaction.

My assessment is about a 16 in the "S" preference.

Lance demands clarity. There has to be a reason for everything and he likes to move through things step-by-step. When we are engaging in any activity, it is very important to him that I know what we are doing and where we are going. Otherwise he becomes anxious and jumpy—not fun with such a big guy.

Once Lance knows something, he never forgets. Balls, cones, barrels, and poles can, at first, be a problem for him. But once he investigates and no longer feels threatened by them, he loves to play with the objects and remembers them each time he sees them.

Lance loads in a trailer like a champ. Trailers don't stress him out and he is happy to stand and graze until asked to move in, which he does comfortably.

My assessment is about an 18-T preference.

It's important that I mention I am an 18-F. I would like nothing better than to hang out, cuddle, and be the center of Lance's world. But that is not Lance's preferred mode. He has a giant heart, but he just doesn't express it in ways that are familiar to me. This attribute is excellent for caretakers who step into his space. He isn't much for coddling.

When Lance goes out to the herd, he goes towards them but doesn't move into them. He does what he had planned to do and can't be bothered with whatever activities his herd mates are engaging in unless he wants to join them in those activities.

In the round pen with clients he is also often seen as aloof and unattached, especially when the person is outwardly emotional. Even in the midst of a client's emotional outpouring, he will push the client to move through it and come to resolution.

Grooming is not Lance's favorite activity. If it needs to happen he likes it to be done quickly, appreciating the scratches and love more than anything else.

I often think I hear Lance saying, "It's my way or the highway." Considering his size, it is imperative that I am clear with my own boundaries. When asking something new of him, I need to ask in an invitational manner. And when he resists, I must hold my ground, otherwise he loses respect and makes his own plans.

My assessment is about a 17-P preference.

Lance is messy and doesn't care that he is. When he eats, it goes everywhere. If he bumps into something and it falls, he could care less. If the water bucket is dirty, he still drinks. And when he stands in the stall, he is not particular about where he does his business.

Lance always loves his food, but if it doesn't come at the same time each day, he doesn't throw a fit. When working in the arena with other horses and handlers, he doesn't care what order they walk in or who is first. He is pretty laid back and takes things in stride.

Lance is an ESTP.
Sara Sherman (ENFP), Brainerd, Minnesota
www.DiscoveryHorse.com

 Spot

A Twenty-Three-Year-Old Spotted Appaloosa Gelding

I partnered with Spot for about a year.

Spot was my break-in horse. As a person who had no horse experience, I was blessed to work with Spot while he was visiting Lil Bit North ranch. Spot is a horse that Melisa has known since he was a weanling and she knew it would be very difficult for a newbie to get into what she called "a horse wreck" with him.

My initial objective was to gain ground work skills, and in keeping with that objective, I worked with Spot in the round pen, groomed him, and walked him. I feel that

Spot is a mixture of personalities. He can be incredibly focused, especially when it comes to getting a chance to eat. He can also be a prankster. One of my favorite stories about his prankster ways is that on my first solo experience of round-penning him, we ended up round-penning each other.

I found Spot to be inquisitive. He was quick in sizing the situation up, yet he was an easygoing guy. When I first worked with him, he allowed me to do things he wasn't especially fond of, like grooming. Even when grooming him at liberty, he was tolerant. My favorite activity with him was to hang out after we had done other things, while he noshed his way up and down the driveway. It was a perfect time for me to settle in as well.

If I were to anthropomorphize Spot, I would think of him as the patient grandfather who knows a lot about the world, keeps to himself, is not easily fazed, is exceptionally pragmatic, and who occasionally pulls a coin out of my ear. He would be a great grandpa to hang out with.

I would consider Spot at about a 6-I.

Spot was fairly low key and without what I would consider a big or loud energetic presence. He did not whinny or run to the fence when he saw me coming like many of the other horses at the ranch. He was courteous, yet aloof. He let me know that he was present, took things in, and then sauntered over to me. Spot conserved his energy instead of racing around. He did not require a lot of space and generally allowed me to come close to him.

Spot was not what I would consider a socializer. When he was stalled near most horses, he stood near the wall the farthest from other horses. That said, I did notice that when he was put out in the adjacent paddock to Bali, a horse he knew well, he was not all that far on the other side of the fence from him. He knew he was there to provide a stabilizing influence for Bali and played that role well.

I would probably put Spot at a 12-S.

In terms of the "N" versus the "S," it is difficult for me to read how Spot would act in terms of needing facts versus imagining possibilities. I have assigned him a 12-S, mostly because I see him as a switch-hitter depending on the circumstances. He was a combination of practical and imaginative. He could amuse himself. For instance, when I groomed him, he loved checking out the brushes and other items in the tack box. One could say that he was gathering information about each of the tools, taking his time as opposed to just giving them a sniff and being done with it. It was almost like a person who wants to know where the brush has been and who else it has been used on.

Spot was also imaginative. He had a reputation of being a breakout artist. He also had the ability to turn a situation into an opportunity for being amusing, like when he decided I needed to be round-penned.

Because he seemed like such a down-to-earth type of being, I would give him an edge on the S side, rather than splitting it down the middle.

My assessment is that Spot is a 13-T.

I did not consider Spot to be a touchy-feely kind of guy, but he was incredibly considerate and tolerant. He seemed to be saying, "Well, this is the kind of thing one does in life." He was not heavily analytical. He was present, but I wouldn't call him emotionally available. If I were to pour out my heart to him, I could almost imagine him putting his hoof up to his mouth and making a quip like, "Hmm, seems like you got yourself into a quandary," as opposed to running up to me and giving me the giant bear hug and telling me, "Everything will be all right."

Spot is a 17-J.

Spot kept his stall pretty neat and poops in just one location, whereas many of his stall mates pooped all over their stalls. He was methodical while he noshed up or down the driveway. He tended to eat in a small area, almost as if there were zones he should eat in. And as he ate, he moved up or down rather than from left to right. When he was in his stall, he ate somewhat predictably. Rather than eating hurriedly, he ate slowly and steadily.

If Spot did not want to do something, he could dig in and become nearly unmovable. When I first started working with Spot, we had many a conversation in which I pointed out to him that it couldn't always be his way or the highway. He was a great teacher in leadership skills.

Spot is an ISTJ.
BB Harding (INFJ), Longmont, Colorado
www.AHorseandAWizard.com

◉ WILMA

A Twenty-Four-Year-Old Friesian Mare

We have been partners for eleven years.

I knew the moment we met that Wilma and I were destined to be together. She was perfect for me: not very big, as Friesians go, just a quarter of an inch above fifteen hands; calm and obedient; and she loved being groomed. It didn't matter to me that she had never been ridden and had spent the first twelve years of her life making babies. She moved from broodmare to riding horse with quiet aplomb, and she has always impressed me with her thoughtful nature.

When I joined the EGC coaching program, she leaped into that new career with the same calm attention to detail that she gives to everything else. She is, in a word, unflappable.

Wilma is the most popular of my horses in the EGC work. She approaches each client in exactly the way that is needed. She's their rock, a solid foundation on which they can build their confidence, fill their heart, and move toward a better future. And she does it with her own huge heart wide open. It may look like not much is happening, but this is a horse with great depth of feeling. That becomes very apparent the longer you are in her presence. She's subtle and she is fully present for every person. She is always the first to put her hoof up to work, and if one of the other horses is chosen, she will still work it from the sidelines. She knows her worth.

My assessment is about an 8-I preference.

Although not naturally effusive, Wilma is the definite leader of our small band of horses, a job she performs with subtlety and grace. No loud noises or huge gestures for this lady. A flick of an ear from her will move the most belligerent of herdmates.

Wilma prefers calm and order, and she does not need to be in the middle of the action. She will watch the antics of the other horses from the sidelines, enjoying their hijinks but seldom actively participating. The others can occasionally convince her to go for a little run but before long, she's back to grazing and leaving the others to their silliness. It's not her age. She has always been this way—willing to leave the herd and be with people, standing alone in the barn for grooming, or going for a ride down the road.

Wilma is about a 16-S preference.

Wilma is a thinker. It's one of the things that makes her calm on the trail. This is a horse who, for the entire first half of her life, left the farm maybe once a year to go to the foal judging and then returned to the quiet of her stall and pasture. She had very little to go on regarding the outside world, and yet, I would trust her anywhere. She looks, evaluates the situation, asks questions, and thinks. Then she responds. She very seldom reacts.

She also behaves as a thinker with those who come for sessions. She observes them closely and then chooses how she will approach the situation to help her client find the best possible solution.

She is about an 18 on the scale for the "F" preference.

Wilma's heart is huge. She loves people and is always willing to give her all. In typical "I" fashion, she thrives on one-on-one attention. She is always happy to see us when we come to the barn—ears up, soft-eyed, sending love our way.

Wilma works extremely well with clients who have issues around worthiness or who need to receive loving feedback. She will wrap her neck around a client and let them sob into her big body. She takes it all in and gives the client the place of safety and comfort they need. She seems to know exactly when to step in and give them all of her heart in support so that they can tap into the strength at their root to take the steps to make the change necessary for their transformation.

She is about a 15-J.

When I first met Wilma, I was amazed at the orderliness of her stall. The manure went into the corner farthest from the manger. She shares a large common area with another horse now and she always goes to "her" corner for her grain.

She knows which feet get picked up in which order for cleaning and if it changes for some reason, her discomfort is easily felt. At those times, she seems to be saying, "Don't you want *this* hoof now?"

Once she has completed her evaluation of a situation with clients, her methods are very precise. She knows what to do, how much to do, and in what order to do it to achieve the optimum result in service to the client. The magic is that she does it all with so much heart.

Wilma is an ISFJ.

Ashara Morris (INFP), Elizabeth, Colorado
www.HarmonysHeartCoaching.com

○ Mac

An Eleven-Year-Old Paint Gelding

We have been partners for three years.

When I was first introduced to Mac four years ago, it was with this warning: "He is very aggressive and he bites. Go into his stall with caution."

One look into those big brown eyes and I was hooked. He was aggressive, but from the beginning I believed it to be a remnant of his past as a professional show horse, one that is kept stalled and taken out to work and put back when the job is done. It was also his way of getting attention, like a human child who thinks that the only way to get someone to pay attention to him is to do something bad. When the teeth came out I would push his face away and just start scratching. His favorite itchy spots are neck and rump and he will place himself where he wants to be scratched. I won him over very quickly that way, and his aggressive tendencies are gone.

We began our partnership while I was in training for my EGC career. With his tendencies toward humans being not so nice, he was not used in the program. I felt such a connection toward him that I would ask to be partnered with him for my personal work. By assisting me in my healing, he showed that he had a great capacity to try and to give. I find that people gravitate toward him, perhaps because he has kind of a charming "bad boy" persona and is also a bit goofy at times.

I believe Mac to be a 6-I.

Although he loves to be the center of attention, Mac seems to get overwhelmed when the energy around him is high. Having been a show horse for many years, he is used to being in crowds and performing in an arena, but those situations tend to be controlled. He tends to gravitate toward energies that are calm and peaceful. He is also very attached to one person—me—and has suffered from separation anxiety when I have been away for a few days. He goes off his feed, becomes very depressed, and pouts for a few days when I come home.

   The first time I attempted to turn him out in a pasture with another horse, he ran away from it. The other horse was very outgoing and was trying to introduce himself, but Mac seemed to think he was being chased and kept running away. He tried to hide behind me so the other horse would not be able to get to him. He now has his own pony who caters to his need for some quiet.

I would say he is a 12-N.

Mac is quick to assess anything new or different that enters his space. He knows when to assert himself into your space and when to stay away. He is not the type of horse that wants to be first in line, but he won't stand back if no one else takes the lead.

   He gets excited when he gets something right. At times he appears reserved, cold, or unresponsive, but he is actually hypersensitive to signals of rejection from those for whom he cares.

He is at least a 16-T.

Mac knows what he knows and he gets out of sorts when something changes. When he is in a riding arena, he will do whatever is asked as long as it makes sense to him.

For instance, when I held an American flag while sitting on his back, Mac stood quietly as long as someone was standing on the ground next to me. When the person attempted to walk away, Mac believed that they were holding the flag, and when he realized he and I were holding the flag, it no longer made sense to him. He totally lost composure and I had to drop the flag. As soon as he realized that we were not responsible for it, he was fine. Each time we attempted to carry the flag, the same thing happened. As long as he believed someone else was holding it, life was good.

That same day, I attempted to ride him over some obstacles in a wooded area outside the fenced arena. He went willingly at first and seemed to enjoy the change of scenery. But he became agitated very quickly. Agitation then progressed to overwhelm, at which point he made it clear that he wanted to go back to the fenced arena where I had just gotten him to put all four feet on an eighteen-inch pedestal and walk up to a person shooting a starter pistol that shoots loud blanks.

Lastly, I believe Mac to be around a 13-J.

Mac enjoys order and boundaries in his work, and while he tolerates change, he prefers everything stay the same. Mac likes routine and prefers to have a plan. He loves performing predetermined patterns. He approaches work seriously but also knows when it is okay to play. When he's not working, he is pretty laid back, preferring to just to be with his pony or graze in his pasture.

Mac is an INTJ.
Lisa Martin (E/INFJ), Bethel, NC
www.TrottingForward.com

⊙ LITTLE C

A Twenty-One-Year-Old Paso Fino Mare

We have been on this journey for fifteen years.

Ever since reading Walter Farley's *The Black Stallion*, I had dreamed of having a black horse. I fell in love with Little C at first sight. That love was not reciprocated initially. I spent months sitting just inside her stall door, reading, while she stood in the opposite corner, head down, butt towards me. She was not threatening, just disgruntled that I was in her space. Occasionally, she tilted her head ever so slightly and looked at me out her left eye, only to look away if I made eye contact or spoke.

It took an abundance of patience, understanding, and determination to earn her trust and her partnership. I had her for more than a year before I "caught" her lying down.

She is highly aware of everything around her and it's been said that she knows what's going to happen long before it happens. She is the watcher and alpha mare of my herd. I treasure each time she approaches me or allows me to sit with her while she is lying down.

Little C and I are still developing an EGC partnership. At first, she seemed disinterested and was willing to let another herd member step up and partner with me. In the pasture, she appears quiet and stoic. Many people are drawn to her, only to be quietly dismissed as she walks away.

As I become more aware, I am finding that Little C's work is very subtle and often done at a distance. She lends a strong, feminine, motherly support to the client.

My assessment is about an 8-I preference.

Little C is very standoffish. She does not come up to greet people or horses. She is not very social and very much prefers one-on-one interaction. In a herd of eight horses, she has just one partner she stays with. Even as alpha mare, her signals are at a distance, and when she has to make close contact to get her point across, it is quick and to the point.

She is about a 16-S preference.

Little C is very based in reality and fact. She takes in all of the details of her surroundings. She is not a horse you can make do something. She prefers that you do things a specific way, and if you stray from that, you might just get "the look" from her.

I'd say she is about a 17-T preference.

Little C is very analytical. I took her to a two-week Parelli clinic in 2006. One of the exercises we were given was to *send* the horses into the trailer instead of *leading* them into the trailer. I tried to send that mare into the trailer for hours. We had no previous trailer loading issues, but she would only put two feet in it and then back out. Each time she did that, she also looked around the side of the trailer. I finally gave up and walked her back to her pen.

That evening, it came to me. She wouldn't get in the trailer because it wasn't hooked up to a truck! The trailer was a permanent fixture used as a training device and was very secure. But it wasn't going anywhere, so why should she get in it? When we were leaving, the trainers actually walked me to my truck and trailer thinking I was going to have issues loading. Little C saw that my trailer was hooked to my truck and jumped right in without being led in.

Little C is an 18-J preference.

Little C is a very tidy mare. She poops in one spot when stalled or in the pasture and has even trained the other horses to do so, too.

She is very aware of time. When I first got her, I was feeding at approximately the same time each night. The first night I was late, my kids said that she had started pacing the fence at the normal feeding time, so I started paying attention to that. Sure enough, she started making her way to her stall at 5:00 p.m., and if there wasn't food in the feeder, she began pacing the fence. She prefers it if you follow a routine with her.

This mare is very serious and down-to-earth. She has very little play drive. Little C likes to know what her job is and then go to it. She needs purpose when asked to do something, especially if it is out of the norm.

Little C is an ISTJ.

MICHELLE SIDUN (E/ISTJ), RAWLINS, WYOMING
www.ThroughtheHorse.com

SIR WILLOUGHBY, AKA "WILLY"

A Twenty-Two-Year-Old Chestnut Appendix Quarter Horse Gelding

Willy and I have been partners for about five years.

Willy was donated to me in 2010 by one of my very best horse trainer friends. Willy was one of her favorites. Even Willy's full name, Sir Willoughby, denotes a discerning personality. If he were human, he would be a jock who just likes to hang out with a few buddies and watch football. He has been a show or lesson horse his whole life, is good at his job, and loves it.

Willy is a 9-I.

Willy has a definite boundary bubble and if you are another horse, you had better stay out of his space. He has one good friend (who is an ENFP), but he does not care if he is with other horses in a lesson or show.

Willy stands with his hind end to the door if a crowd of humans comes through the barn. He's great to use for E/I work. He will totally ignore the extraverts if they are chattering or get in his bubble.

Willy doesn't expend any more energy than necessary.

Willy is a 19-S.

As a lesson horse, Willy likes the rider to be very clear with aids. If they are not, he certainly teaches them to be. He prefers STJ riders and competing as a hunter (as opposed to jumper rounds), and he almost always places in the top three.

I have never seen Willy spook. He is black-and-white, practical, sensible, and reliable. As an EGCM horse, he is a great lie detector and gets a kick out of calling bullshit. He is my go-to horse for many experiential exercises.

Willy is an 18-T.

Willy has no patience with emotions. He is okay to be loved on by very few, and when he is okay with it, it is only as long as no one else is watching and a peppermint (not an apple or carrot) is involved. He will sometimes balance chakras, but only the first chakra.

He holds firm to his principles and will absolutely not change his mind if you go against his standards, whether that is with feed, clothes, tack, or riders.

Willy is a 14-J.

Willy likes order and he likes to be on a schedule. If his schedule is changed, he wants to know about it.

His stall is very tidy. He does not step in, lie down in, or spread out his poop. He poops and pees in the same spots in his stall.

Willy likes to get things done in a timely manner.

Willy is an ISTJ.
Harriet Morton (INFJ), Abbeville, South Carolina
www.Cricket-Hollow.com

TRACE

A Six-Year-Old Half-Andalusian, Half Quarter Horse-Appaloosa, Mare

Trace and I have been partners for seven years.

Crosswinds Trace was born at my farm in Pennsylvania. She arrived into the world with innate beauty and strength and a clear sense of who she is. The others in the herd immediately treated her with respect, just like her mom (who was the lead mare).

As a young filly, she liked to be seen, and when she focused her energy on you, it could easily be felt.

Always on alert, Trace often feels like a tight piano string, especially when she is introduced to new surroundings. Her curiosity and keen intelligence were also obvious from the start. If she is bored, she is something of a pest, untying ropes, taking brushes out of bags, and taking tools off four-wheelers when we are repairing fences or gates. Trace has no respect for the space or belongings of others and will take what she wants. She even taught herself to open doors by turning knobs with her mouth, and she has let herself into the tack room more than once.

Her eating habits are quick and to the point: first grain, then hay, then a drink. She is definitely motivated by food, yet she is always neat and orderly and very rarely dirty.

Trace gets bored very easily and is a very quick learner. For example, when teaching her to accept the saddle pad, I let her approach and smell it, then I rubbed her with it and placed it on her back. When I started to do this again, she looked at me as if to say, "Hey, I get it. Can we please move on now to something more interesting?" Not wanting to bore her, I did just that.

Her will and self-preservation are very strong and must be respected if you want her to work for you and not against you.

When coaching clients, Trace is straightforward and prefers to get right to the point. Long stories bore her and inconsistency will not keep her attention. She has been known to nudge people forward after clearing chakras, almost as if to say, "I've done my job, now you do yours."

My assessment is about a 7-E preference.

If not with the herd, Trace stays nearby, always observing. When I walk out to the pasture, she is one of the first to nicker and either walks or trots to me. Often she only wants to make sure that all is well and know what is going on. Then she will go back to the herd.

   Trace enjoys company on her terms. When out on a ride, she will get to know one or two horses and invite them into her herd. She typically is not physically herd-bound and can leave the herd and be on her own, but she prefers to stay in emotional contract.

   When new surroundings or people are introduced, Trace always has to first touch, smell, and cross into your space. She sometimes licks, wanting to be sure you know who she is.

My assessment is about a 15-N preference.

Trace is alert and ever vigilant, especially in new surroundings. She always seems to be anticipating what will happen, casting an eye to the far woods or horizon, aware of plant or branch movement. She notices if an obstacle has been moved.

   She is sensitive and does not like to be corrected, especially when she believes the correction is not justified.

My assessment is about a 12-T preference.

Trace can appear impersonal at times, especially if you don't know her well.

   When in training, she responds best when she is able to understand the criteria and purpose of the exercise. She loves to solve puzzles and can be quite a trickster. She also prefers fairness over harmony, expects to be appreciated for her thought process and try, and learns by touching and looking at obstacles, if possible.

She does like grooming and likes to be fussed over. Because of that, I believe she is not a real high T. She does fall into her F side the more confident and older she becomes.

My assessment is about a 14-J preference.

Trace is very neat and clean. She does not like to get muddy or wet. She prefers a routine (to a point). For instance, she always finishes her grain first. Then she goes on to her hay and cleans up everything. She prefers to learn, be appreciated, and complete her work without dillydallying around. Then she likes to get into the trailer and go home. Sitting around bores her. She wants to complete one task and then move on to another.

Trace is an ENTJ.

Barbara Broxterman (INTP), Williston, Florida
www.WayfindingwithHorses.com

Each person who administers the Equusology instrument will be attempting to be as nonjudgmental or nonbiased as possible. But no matter what type you are, your filters are operating. As you type your horses, it can be enlightening to have someone who knows your horse and who is a different type from you (on the Keirsey Temperament Sorter) also look at the results for comparison feedback.

As stated earlier, each of our Equine Gestalt Coaches who contributed case studies for this book has been trained in using the KTS with humans. They have disclosed their own temperament (at the end of the case study, next to their name) for the sake of transparency.

Equusology can be fun, adding a dimension of understanding for you with your horses. It will also help your riding instructor, barn owner, or employees understand your horses better.

Some readers may desire to dive more deeply into this new field of Equusology and apply this to training. They may also want to use it to gain more clarity about and understanding of clients. Some may just want to know their own horse better. However Equusology is used, better relationships will be the result.

CHAPTER EIGHTEEN

You and Your Horse

YOU HAVE HAD A CHANCE TO TAKE THE KEIRSEY TEMPERAMENT SORTER, complete the Equusology Sorter, and have some fun with your horse doing the exercises to check out your instincts about your horse's type. You have also seen case studies that, hopefully, bring the Equusology Sorter into real-world focus. Now, let's take it all one step further by applying what you have learned in some possible human/horse scenarios.

🐎 SOCIAL EXPERIENCE

Let's look at the social experience with your horse. If you understand the differences between extravert (E) and introvert (I) personalities and apply those principles to you and your horse, you will begin to see your social likes and dislikes, as well as those of your horse. That will help you and your horse become more aligned with each other.

The E human comprises 75% of the general population and the I comprises 25% of the general population.

As an example of this, the extraverted human likes lots of interaction with others, is quite talkative, is energized in the presence of large groups of people, has difficulty spending large quantities of time alone, and is very happy when a lot is going on around them. The extraverted horse likes to be with other horses and can be more vocal with their herd mates than the introverted horses. The E horse does not like to live in isolation or even with only one herd mate. He prefers a lot of action around him for stimulation and likes to have other animals to interact with throughout his day.

The introverted human prefers to hang out with a few close friends, and does fine in a small facility with one other horse person. They tend to speak only when they have something important to say, and is energized when they have quiet time to themselves. The introverted horse has certain horses they like hanging out with, seldom nickers, and seems less anxious when their surroundings are quiet.

So what could be some possibilities to consider? If a human who is an extravert (E) is paired with a horse who is an introvert (I), the two would desire different environments. It is very likely that the E human would gravitate towards horse showing, large group trail riding, or gymkhana events. The I horse would feel anxious and energy-depleted most of the time because of the surroundings his E human places him in. At a show, he would prefer that his stall be in a corner or near a tack stall so he can escape some of the show activity. He would also like it better if his human preferred trail riding with one other horse and rider instead of a group ride.

This scenario doesn't mean the two couldn't be happy and supportive of each other, but what it does mean is that the human could support his horse more fully if he didn't choose a discipline that exposed his horse to overstimulation and allowed the horse enough downtime in quieter environments for reenergizing. Of course, choices about activities and environment are sometimes made before the human understands either their type or the horse's type. In those cases, you can create opportunities for your horse to spend time with one or two congenial horses or give him turn out time in a grassy pasture alone so he can find his source of energy and balance.

◉ LEARNING STYLE

Just as you have your own learning style, your horse has his own, too. You have identified your learning style through your type. Your horse also has a unique style, and this style is important when it comes to training and everyday contact. Our everyday lives are shaped and molded by what we have interest in and how we learn.

S humans and N humans have very different ways of collecting their data. They also have vast differences in what they value and often have differences in how they expose their children to educational experiences.

S humans comprise 75% of the general population versus N humans who comprise 25% of the general population. S humans value experience and the wisdom of the past. They see themselves as realistic and have a lot of respect for those who are willing to do hard work. They rely on details and facts and don't have much tolerance for what they view as nonsense. They feel everyone should learn how to be useful.

S horses learn best when shown skills in small steps. They like the structure and competitiveness of learning a skill well and repeating that skill until they have it perfected. S horses don't mind working hard and sweating, and they do not bore easily.

N humans would describe themselves as seeing possibilities, being imaginative, and being ingenious. They tend to value hunches and a vision for the future. They see possibilities instead of being tied to what is considered by others to be what is a given truth or unavoidable reality at the present moment. N humans often find themselves with a vague sense of dissatisfaction or restlessness because so many of their dreams do not come to fruition quickly.

N horses learn by taking in their surroundings globally. They often miss small details because they are scanning the situation or glancing at many things instead of having a concentrated focus on one or two things. They have exuberance for life.

Let's look at an N human with an N horse and an N human with an S horse. It is very likely that the N human would find excitement in disciplines such as liberty work, fox-hunting, or parades. The N horse could find adventure in having no set routine and no ongoing, repeated practice. Life is more unpredictable for them and they can imagine what is around the bend. At liberty, the N horse could appear brilliant because he prefers that you not expect him to act like everyone else. The N horse that has schooling as a western pleasure horse could easily become bored and display inattentiveness. His lack of attention could be interpreted as a form of disobedience, when in reality, he has only lost his attentiveness because repetitiveness is not his style. He finds his glee moments when he can show his creativity.

Now what if the N human has an S horse? An S horse likes details and thrives on doing a job they have mastered well. They also might look lost without guidance. The S horse could be brilliant if he was schooled as a western pleasure horse and given the time to master his gaits and transitions. In that situation, he would be a content and happy horse.

If you are an S human, how can you support your N horse? If you show your horse, make opportunities for unorganized trail rides or provide extra turnout for your horse in different locations. The biggest thing to remember is that details and structure make you comfortable but bore your horse. He needs experiences that encourage him to be creative and allow him to learn things on his own.

The S human and S horse can partner easily because both are concerned with details and routines. The repetition of drills and practice are calming and welcome, although the SP will need to have freedom in between sessions. The S horse seeks out the details of his human partner's requests, such as height of wrist or pressure point on their side, and appreciates the signals being exactly the same each time they are given. This is also the natural tendency of the S human.

◔ LEARNING STYLE APPLIED TO TRAINING

What might you expect when you apply this in training? Training is centered on our ability to communicate with our horses. Whether human or horse, each student in school has their own learning style. Certain methods reach one horse and leave another confused. And when the horse is confused, the trainer needs to make adjustments, not the horse. When we understand the type preferences, we can move more quickly to success with our methods.

Let's say you are working with a highly extraverted colt. His natural preference is to see and even whinny to all nearby horses and to fret if he cannot see his barn mates. The trainer who understands that this is a basic part of the horse's personality and not misbehavior will work with this preference and not against it. This may mean taking the colt off to a round pen where he cannot see other horses in order to help him concentrate. If done for short periods of time at first, it will not feel so much like punishment. Then the trainer can slowly increase the amount of independent time each day to increase the horse's tolerance. As a reward, the horse could then be turned out to wherever the center of interaction is.

On the other hand, the highly introverted colt will appreciate a solid-sided round pen and major lessons being given with as little noise and distraction around him as possible. Finding a quiet morning or quiet place to work with this colt will help him focus for a longer period of time. Having time alone immediately after an important session, such as first saddling, will allow this colt to integrate the learning, whereas putting him out to pasture with other colts may lessen his retention.

Let's say that the trainer next rides a colt he can clearly see has a learning style of an S—a detail seeker. The trainer normally does warm-up circles and exercises with the colts to start the ride time, but his colt seems nervous and looks everywhere but where he is going when he is in the ring. Knowing he has an S colt, he can save a great deal of time and frustration by allowing the colt ten minutes up front to actually touch and examine the physical objects of interest around him, thereby allowing him to gather details and facts that comfort his need to know before he can concentrate on the lesson.

This need is very different from that of an N colt, who would love the circles, taking in his environment more intuitively. Unlike the S colt, the N colt would not want to be fed the details about objects in the ring.

Reward can be a large part of a trainer's repertoire, and there are many methods for giving horses praise or rewards. The "release" or lack of pressure is a common behavior modification-based reward used for training horses. It is used a lot because it works with most horses as they seek to discover when we will stop pressure on their lead rope or bit and/or the pressure we are exerting with our seat. However, they are experiencing it differently according to their type

For the SP horse, it is freedom he is seeking. The SJ horse understands it as long as it is identical each time it is given, so he can count on the cause and effect being steady. The NF horse goes along with the release but it is not enough. He craves appreciation and will respond to the release even better if intermittent praise (verbally or with a rub on the neck) is added to the training. The NT horse is watching for consistency or inconsistency in your cues and will react by seemingly being set back if he finds a pattern that is incorrect. He will protest with a head shake or tail wring to express his annoyance.

◑ Decision Making

Now that we have looked at the differences in social preferences and learning styles, let's explore how we use our preferences to make decisions. The T is more comfortable making decisions with impersonal or objective judgments while the F encourages feedback from others and takes their logic and feelings into account, thereby making their decisions more personal. The T type would rely on policy, law, and objectivity when making decisions. The F type would be aware of the policy or law but then take extenuating circumstances, personal relationships, or other subjective things into consideration when making their decisions.

Let's look at how this appears in our horses. What decisions do they make? Some are how to react to the daily barn routine. The SJ horse appreciates the order and routine that the barn crew establishes. They seek consistency when it comes to the order in which they and the others are fed and what time feeding occurs. They want to use the pathway to their turnout and they want to be bathed at the same rack every time. This keeps their world orderly and according to plan.

By contrast, the NF is not as interested in the routine as they are in the contact or exchange with the barn workers. The NF relishes being spoken to, patted while their stall is being cleaned, or any other personal attention.

The NT horse is an observer, always watching for changes that are not workable for them. They are not happy when new horses are put in the stall next to them or new barn workers come to work. They will seem aloof and stand-offish while observing it all.

The SP observes, too, but for different reasons. If they observe that a door is left open, they may slip out for a little run around the farm. And if they can shake up the routine, they will. That might include dragging their hay into their waterer to see what will happen.

Understanding the difference between the T and the F seems to be the area of largest misunderstanding because T personalities are often described as being "heartless," "stone-hearted," "cold," "remote," as having "ice in their veins," or as "intellectualizing." You will hear them verbalize what they think. The T horse is a very objective decision maker and shows little subjectivity. He does not display appreciation for lots of hugging and heartfelt emotions from his humans. He will appreciate being in your presence, but not appreciate constant touching or stroking from you.

F personalities are often described as "unable to take a firm stand," "too emotional," "illogical," "fuzzy thinkers," "people who wear their hearts on their sleeves," or "too soft-hearted," and you will hear them verbalize how they feel.

Sometimes the F is seen as more emotionally sensitive than the T, but this is not really the case. The F horse is influenced positively by human touch and physical expression of emotions towards him. When uncertain, they are likely to rely on their person to help them make a good decision. They also take other circumstances into consideration if a decision has to be made that is out of the norm.

Both types can react emotionally with the same intensity. The F person tends to make his emotional reactions very visible, which may make others see him as warmer or more capable of deeper feelings than a T. The T person does not readily display their emotions and are sometimes embarrassed when they do.

A T horse could potentially enjoy being a lesson horse or a dressage horse. They would have been taught what was expected of them before they joined the lesson string or competitive arena and now they would follow established policies and procedures.

How can an F human support a T horse? The human will want lots of physical close-ness to their horse but must remember that their horse doesn't have this need. They can learn to express their connection with their horse in different ways, like placing extra special treats in the feeder after a good ride and staying in their presence, and talking to them.

An F horse could enjoy being a therapy horse and might visibly exhibit devotion and intimacy with their clients.

How can a T human support an F horse? The human will be very objective and may not often express how he feels about his horse to his horse. He will need to remember that his horse needs expressions of connection, appreciation, and affection.

⬤ STRUCTURE

A person who prefers closure in their world is most likely a J while the person who prefers keeping his options open and not making final decisions is most likely a P. The J human makes lots of lists and likes things checked off and completed. He takes those lists seriously and expects others to take them seriously too. The J human pushes for decisions from others. When a J person has made a decision, he feels a sense of completion and satisfaction. A J must complete work before he can take off and have fun. A J is often described by a P as a "stick-in-the-mud" or "too task-oriented."

The J horse has a good work ethic and can appear very settled even as a young horse. He accepts pressure more willingly than the free-spirited P type and shows his spontaneous side after his work is completed.

P humans tend to see deadlines as a small buzz that can be turned on or off easily. They want to start a project at or near the set deadline, not have it completed by then. They live their lives without a sense of urgency. Ps hold out on making decisions and they usually have a list of reasons why they haven't made them, but internally, they may actually feel uneasy after they make decisions because there are always additional things to consider. Ps like to have fun and can rest or play before work without feeling guilty.

The P horse has a more laid-back attitude than the J horse because he lives his life in more of a "wait and see" attitude. He can find fun in almost everything and is best at his job if he views the job as fun. The P horse often looks like he has all the time in the world.

A J human would probably enjoy the discipline of competitive trail riding, racing, or showing with their equine partner. All of these disciplines require planning ahead, have fixed rules, and are performed with some sense of urgency. What if the J human is paired with a P horse? The P horse would prefer few to no rules and much more flexibility within his schedule than the J horse. He may even feel a cue and seem slow to respond when, in fact, he is not expressing slowness but just a relaxed response. The high J horse will make prompt departures and react to cues on time but gets anxious if waiting for his turn to perform.

You could support your P horse by allowing him to play a little and show his personality while going down the trail or allow him to check out the show grounds with you in the saddle after the completion of a class in a more relaxed way, without time parameters.

The P human does not keep to a set schedule as much as his J counterpart. This can be in keeping with horses' emotional systems because horses do not wear watches or track time concretely. However, they do appreciate feeding, stall cleaning, and paddock turn out to be done regularly and may become anxious if the P human is too lax in responding to these basic needs. The J horse will be less forgiving of these habits than the P horse who is already more "go with the flow" in attitude. The J horse is seeking comfort by paying attention to the barn schedule and routine. The P horse less so.

Clearly, the discussion about human and horse type combinations could be endless because there are so many possible combinations that are worth examining. Taking into consideration the strength of each number and the preferences our horses are exhibiting will go a long way to a closer and more sincere bond between you and your horse. While every personality—both human and equine—is unique, certain match-ups between humans and horses work with ease while others require a bit more understanding and the willingness to make allowances. Just as in human relationships, opposites in human-horse relationships often attract and work well, with each balancing the strengths and weaknesses of the other. By paying attention to the typology of both partners, lessons can be learned and enjoyable times together can be enhanced.

CHAPTER NINETEEN

Sliding to a Stop

THIS BOOK ONLY TOUCHES THE SURFACE OF THIS TOPIC. WE HOPE IT LED YOU to a place of appreciation for your own temperament and the temperaments of those around you, both human and equine. Every temperament and its degree of preference is the platform from which the personality develops, the values are formed, and the self emerges. As individuals, we then layer on different experiences, including those impacted by who raised us and how we were raised.

Each life is precious. It is our intent that by reading this book, the door will be opened for you to see another way of looking at yourself with appreciation and in gratitude.

Our horses also have lives impacted by how they were treated in their formative years. When a colt is born, if it is imprinted and handled by a human partner who has raised foals and is confident doing so, that colt will have a very different experience from the colt with a novice horseman who is learning as they go along while experimenting with how to handle a new foal. And those different experiences will prepare them for life.

Even the attitude of the mare toward her caretakers can influence how a foal responds to humans as she imprints that attitude, positive or negative.

If a foal was born and had little contact with humans for the first two years of his life while turned out on a large working ranch, he will see life from a highly different perspective than a foal who is the sole entertainment on a small family farm and is handled daily. But even with these obvious differences in experience and shaping in their young lives, the two horses will still have more similarities than differences wherever their innate temperament matches. This reminds us that the horses' personalities are built on a platform of their innate preferences even though their life experiences may differ widely. If both horses are SJ by type, you will see many areas in which they learn or approach new situations and even manage their stall care for themselves in the same way.

If the two foals above differ in temperament—say one is an SJ and the other an SP—the former will be born with a desire to be of service and learn by routine and repeated expectations while the other will be born for adventure. They will be very different horses to raise and train, and they will have very different needs.

Our equine partners are hugely adaptable and forgiving souls, so whatever and however you partner with your horses, we hope you see them more fully as who they are.

Happy Trails.

We would love to invite you to join our webinars or group discussion conference calls to share your thoughts about this topic or to learn more about this new approach.

To find our calendar, go to

www.Equusology.com or
www.TouchedbyaHorse.com and click Equusology

Additional materials on Equusology are available as audio lectures on this topic.

If you are interested in bringing your horse to a clinic weekend to learn more about communicating together on the ground and in the saddle according to type, see our clinics page or go to www.TheHorseConnectionLLC.com.

Your feedback is always welcome. Please leave feedback at info@Equusology.com. Thank you for joining us.

Melisa Pearce
Carolyn Fitzpatrick

About the Authors

🐎 CAROLYN FITZPATRICK

Carolyn Fitzpatrick has the need to be around horses like others have a need for the air they breathe. A lifelong horsewoman, Carolyn is a Certified Equine Gestalt Coaching Method practitioner and the creator of the Trust-Based Equine Partnership Training Method.

Combining her degrees in psychology and education and certification as a family mediator with her love for the language of equus, Carolyn teaches in a cooperative manner so that horse and human learn to dance through life together with a stronger and deeper level of mutual understanding. Carolyn also assists others in determining their horse's personality preferences through trainings at her facility, Bellamy Farms, and at clinics across the continental US.

Carolyn Fitzpatrick has cocreated Equusology with Melisa Pearce with the hope and expectation that it will improve the relationship between horses and their human partners everywhere.

Carolyn and her husband live on Bellamy Farms in Virginia and enjoy distant trail riding. To learn more about Carolyn and her equine workshops, upcoming events, and retreats, please visit her website, www.TheHorseConnectionLLC.com. Find her on Facebook at: www.Facebook.com/TheHorseConnection.

◑ MELISA PEARCE

Melisa Pearce is the founder of Touched by a Horse® and the creator of the Equine Gestalt Coaching Method®. A lifelong horsewoman, Melisa earned a master's degree in social work and began creating her unique therapeutic approach to emotional healing through interactive work with both a therapist and a therapy horse in 1982.

Melisa studied with David Keirsey and became certified in the administration and interpretation of the Keirsey Temperament Sorter about the time she was finishing her master's degree. During her many years of using the Keirsey Temperament Sorter, she has found it to be a profoundly useful tool for understanding human preferences and behavior. When she began to see the same kind of temperament preferences in horses, she realized that the horse-human relationship could be enhanced by expanding the concept of temperament to the equine realm. She is the cocreator of the Equusology Sorter with Carolyn Fitzpatrick.

Melisa Pearce is the author of the inspirational card deck, *Whispers from a Horse's Heart,* and the novel, *Eponalisa.* She also coauthored the book *Games People Play with Horses,* has created a series of audio recordings, and is editor of *Touched by a Horse Equine Coaching Stories,* Volumes 1 and 2.

Melisa lives near Elizabeth, Colorado, with her husband, Dane Cheek, her herd of equine partners, and a veritable menagerie of animals.

You can find more information about Melisa Pearce, her groundbreaking work, and her certification program at:

www.TouchedbyaHorse.com
www.EGCMethod.com
www.EquiSpiritual.com
www.Eponalisa.com